THE MESSAGE
OF SAINT JOHN

THE MESSAGE
OF SAINT JOHN

The Spiritual Teaching
of the Beloved Disciple

By
Rev. Thomas E. Crane

ALBA · HOUSE NEW · YORK

SOCIETY OF ST. PAUL, 2187 VICTORY BLVD., STATEN ISLAND. NEW YORK 10314

Library of Congress Cataloging in Publication Data

Crane, Thomas E
    The message of St. John.

    1. Bible. N.T. Johannine literature—Criticism,
interpretation, etc. 2. Bible. N.T. Johannine literature—Theology. I. Title.
BS2601.C68   225.6   80-11779
ISBN 0-8189-0402-X

Nihil Obstat:
Daniel V. Flynn, J.C.D.
Censor Librorum

Imprimatur:
Joseph T. O'Keefe
Vicar General, Archdiocese of New York
Feb. 22, 1980

The Nihil Obstat and Imprimatur are
a declaration that a book or pamphlet is considered
to be free from doctrinal or moral error. It it is not implied
that those who have granted the Nihil Obstat and
Imprimatur agree with the contents,
opinions or statements expressed.

Designed, printed and bound in the United States of
America by the Fathers and Brothers of the
Society of St. Paul, 2187 Victory Boulevard,
Staten Island, New York, 10314, as part of their
communications apostolate.

    2 3 4 5 6 7 8 9 (Current Printing: first digit).

DEDICATION

To Seminarians, priests and sisters
who have shared with me the
joy of discovering
God's word.

TABLE OF CONTENTS

INTRODUCTION

"Remain in him now, little ones
so that, when he reveals himself,
we may be fully confident
and not retreat in shame
at his coming" (1 Jn 2:28).

We have moved away in recent years from the former practice of grouping together the four Gospels as historical records, and using them as a base for reconstructing a biography of Jesus. The literary and theological aspects of the Gospels are more in the foreground of our interest now, and the special plan and message of each evangelist is becoming more evident. It is for these reasons that we tend now to group the New Testament writings primarily according to their common authors, rather than merely according to their literary forms, as was the practice before. This is why, instead of speaking in a general way about "Gospels and Epistles," we speak rather about the Synoptic, Pauline and Johannine strands of the NT. The unity of each of these sets of writings comes from the unity of the mind that produced them.

Yet, this unity is not primarily a matter of whether or not the inspired writers of these books agree in details of history, or to what extent we can reconcile them with each other as historical records. Rather, the essentially theological and spiritual character of all the NT writings is becoming more clear to us, as we recognize the special thrust of each of these theological strands of the apostolic Gospel.

In the light of these factors, along with the new versions of the Bible which are available to us now, and of the renewed emphasis on the Liturgy of the Word, we are drawing more from the Scriptures as a principal source of spiritual nourishment. In all of this we are moving toward a revival of interest in the biblical spirituality which was a common feature of the early Church's life-style.

We know that theological specialists give long and sometimes very confusing explanations of what spirituality is, and especially of what they mean by biblical spirituality. However, for the sake of a brief working definition, we can say that spirituality is people's experience of God in their lives, and the way in which they respond to this experience. This means that there is no such thing as spirituality in the abstract; it is always in people, something that appears in people's lives, and in their everyday activity, as well as in their progressive religious growth over a period of years.

When we talk specifically about biblical spirituality, of either the Old or New Testament, we can study the religious experience of the various people who are represented in the Bible. Thus we can speak of such prominent persons as Abraham, Moses, Jeremiah in the Old

Testament, or Mary, Paul or Peter in the New. As a matter of fact, some theologians speak of the spirituality, or the religious experience, of Jesus himself. However, Jesus is so unique and so different from the others that this is really a whole theological study in itself (Christology), so that we would have to devote whole volumes to this, which whould take us beyond the limits of this present study.

Nevertheless, these reflections will follow a special plan. Instead of ranging across both Testaments of the Bible to study the spirituality and religious experience of various persons, we shall concentrate here on a much narrower section of the Bible, and limit our study to the teaching of Saint John, the Beloved Disciple. We shall work on the principle that this Apostle's spirituality was formed by his experience of having been chosen and taught by the Word made Flesh, and that he has pondered this experience for many years. What we have in the Johannine section of the NT, therefore, is the fruit of his mature and profound reflections, which he has passed on to his followers.

Altogether, the NT contains five books which come under the heading of "Johannine Literature," i.e. the Gospel According to John, the First, Second and Third Epistles of John, and the Book of Revelation, or, as it used to be called in some older versions of the Bible, the Apocalypse. The Second and Third Epistles are both brief, and they do not give us much information about the Apostle's spiritual teaching, so we will not consider them here. This leaves us with the project of exploring the Fourth Gospel, the First Epistle and Revelation, in order to discover what the Beloved Disciple has learned from his experience of God in Jesus, and how he passes on his interpretation of it, to others.

So we are not looking primarily at the personality of Saint John, but we are interested in learning how he interprets his experience of knowing God from his association with Jesus. We need, therefore, to become accustomed to listening, so to speak, to his voice (since these biblical messages were intended originally to be heard by groups of listeners, rather than read privately by individuals). This will bring us to acquire a unified and coherent understanding of his style of speaking and teaching, in order to grasp the special message that he has to offer his friends, about Jesus and his Gospel of Eternal Life.

1

THE JOHANNINE CHURCH

> ". . .then you will know the truth,
> and the truth will make you free" (Jn 8:32).

The Setting

In order to focus our study we need to make some preliminary points about the time and place in which the Johannine teaching came to have its present written form. In this regard we follow the mainstream of New Testament commentators who consider that the center of the Johannine teaching and spirituality is Ephesus, the grand and imposing city of the Roman Empire which rests gracefully on the western coast of Asia Minor (present-day Turkey), overlooking the Aegean Sea. If we would go Ephesus today, we could walk through the impressive marble ruins which show a blending of Mediterranean climate, Greek architecture and Roman government. Among these ruins there is the shell of a disused Christian basilica dedicated to St. John; on the wall of this ruined church is a new-looking marble plaque, which says, in Latin, "In this place, the site of the ecumenical council of Ephesus (431 A.D.), Pope Paul VI prayed, 1967." Some few hundreds of yards away, still in the area, on a hilltop, is a little stone cottage with a chapel inside, and known as "Mary's house." We are in a place which has preserved the memory of John and Mary, from the first century! The Ecumenical Council of Ephesus occurred in the place in which Mary was reputed to have lived in the care of Saint John, who took her to his charge at Calvary.

So Ephesus is the place of the Johannine Church. The Christian tradition also holds that Saint John died at a very old age—the last of the apostles to die, although we have no specific account of his death.

This brings us to consider the date of origin of the Johannine Literature. The mainstream of opinion holds that these documents reflect the situation of the Johannine Church in Ephesus during the time of the Roman emperor Domitian (81-96 A.D.). During these years the still-emerging infant Church was moving to a new stage of maturity, which was the post-apostolic age. The original Apostles, whose kerygmatic witness had converted the crowds since the first Pentecost some sixty-five years before, were dead by now. The Christians of Ephesus had been fortunate because their city had received visits from not only the mother of Jesus and the Beloved Disciple, but also from Paul, and possibly from Peter and Luke as well. But now, a new generation has come along, and new troubles are pressing upon the Christians of Ephesus.

These pressures come from several sources. First of all, there are still unconverted Jews who resent Christianity in spite of the fact that Christians claim a spiritual affinity with Judaism. There is also the pagan hellenistic and Roman society with its idols, its earthy rituals and its polytheism. A new problem has arisen because the emperor has demanded that his subjects salute him as Master and God. For most of the subjects of the empire, with their polytheistic life-style, such a demand causes no great difficulty, and even simplifies the role of the emperor as head of both state and religion. Jews object however, because of their monotheistic religion, but they manage to find ways of avoiding confrontation. But now the Christians have a problem too, because the emperor demands for himself a form of religious loyalty which they give to God alone.

Another problem facing the Johannine church is internal, i.e. the problem of incipient heresy. It is becoming more and more imperative to take a stand on whether Jesus is a man of God, or whether he is God as man. The earlier apostolic preachers and witnesses had spoken about Jesus as the Suffering Servant, the Son of Man, the Son of David, the Messiah, the Stone rejected by the builders, etc. But now people are agitating the question whether Jesus is truly as divine as Jahweh whom he called his Father. Some claim that they are no less Christian because they deny that he is. Besides this, there is another group on the opposite end of the spectrum, who hold that Jesus was not fully human, but only a sort of super-spirit or a phantasm, which God inhabited temporarily in order to let people see him visibly. These problems now threaten to split the Church's unity of faith, and so they demand a firm resolution which can claim to rest on apostolic authority.

This is the setting in which the followers of the Beloved Disciple remember the teaching of their venerated patriarch. We also hold that the Johannine Literature, as we have it now, represents several levels of authorship. It represents the person of Jesus, his words and his works; it represents also the teaching of John the Apostle, the Beloved Disciple who is the brother of James and the other son of Zebedee. John has reflected for many years on the privileged experience of knowing the Lord face to face; he has worked consistently to interpret this experience to his Christian followers, explaining it to them from his memory and from his imagination, repeating at length the words of Jesus as they still lingered in his hearing and in his memory, and passing them on to his colony of Ephesian Christian followers.

But John is dead, and it is now the group of his followers who wish to preserve the Apostle's teaching, since it is their direct link with the source and object of their faith. It is now the disciple-evangelist, a friend and follower of Saint John the Apostle, who undertakes the project of putting the Apostle's teaching into a written form, especially as it relates to the special problems which now press on the Ephesian church.

The Literature

So we distinguish the author from the writer; the author and source of the message is John, the Apostle and Beloved Disciple. The writer, whose name we do not know, but whose hand we can see, is a follower of the Apostle; we can call him the disciple-evangelist. The disciple-evangelist probably wrote the First Epistle of John before writing the Fourth Gospel; we hold this opinion because both documents are similar in style, vocabulary and purpose, but the terminology of the Epistle is less clear and definite than that of the Gospel According to John.

The disciple-evangelist probably produced both of these documents after the death of the Apostle. Then, after both the epistle and the gospel came to be written in turn, another disciple of John came along and revised the gospel by adding a few sections, including the last chapter (21), which is an appendix. This last disciple we call the disciple-redactor. In addition, there is still another follower of the Apostle, who seems to have had the same name (John), and who is also Jewish, but who has a very different style of speaking and writing. This other member of the Johannine community is the one whom we recognize as the author of the puzzling and even bizarre work called the Book of Revelation (this is the English equivalent of the Greek word "apocalypse"). This Book of Revelation is, therefore, influenced by the teaching of the Apostle, but somewhat less directly. It may have been composed in parts or stages; one school of thought suggests that three short works have been combined to form this present book. In any case, we take it as also a partial reflection of the teaching of Saint John, composed perhaps about the same time as the epistle and the gospel, i.e. about the end of the first Christian century, or about 95 A. D.

This means that, even though there have been several hands at work here, there is still an underlying unity in the teaching, as well as in the style, the vocabulary and the basic purpose. This unity we attribute to Saint John the Apostle, and this is the unified message which we intend to study in these reflections.

When we compare the Johannine Literature with the Synoptic Gospels or with the Pauline Writings, we notice a combination of basic sameness of faith and witness, and of specific differences in literary form and theological emphasis. These special emphases are the unique contribution of the Beloved Disciple, to the New Testament. It is clear from the beginning that John is not presenting either an unfounded fantasy, or a detailed historical record, in the modern sense of the term. He is notoriously vague and slippery on details of time and place, although he shows such a detailed knowledge of history and geography, that he obviously speaks from the memory of his personal experience. We also notice that John often repeats the same essential message, varying the ways in which he expresses it.

We can see that this teacher is not preoccupied with recording past history in the contemporary technical sense of the term; rather he is witnessing to a mystery, an act of God which has come from heaven and eternity to earth in time, becoming flesh in order to offer to men an unexpected, unmerited and unimaginable gift, an invitation to share in God's own eternal divine life. This is the wonder that John declares: "we saw his glory;" and "what was from the beginning, what we have heard . . . seen with our eyes . . . looked upon . . . and our hands have touched . . . the word of life . . . What we have seen and heard we proclaim in turn to you so that you may share life with us" (1 Jn 1:1-3).

In the writings of Eusebius, a church historian from the fourth century A.D., (Heb 6:14-7), we have a quotation from Clement of Alexandria to the effect that the Fourth Gospel is "*pneumatikon*" or "spiritual", whereas the Synoptic Gospels are "*somatika*" or "material." In order to understand this we need to do more than merely to translate the Greek words to English equivalents. It means that John's style of language and his level of thought are directed not so much at what we can know in sensible terms, or by sense-experience, as to what we can learn to perceive by the insight of faith. John's language is the language of nuance, symbolism, suggestion and intuition. He does not spell out details, but he points out directions. He is not at all a complete biographer or a precise historian, or a systematic theologian. He is a witness to the pure apostolic faith, who describes heaven and earth, time and eternity, in the same breath.

As we become accustomed to the Johannine style of language, we will find that it is remarkably consistent. John stays on this exalted and intuitive level; he demands that his disciples stay there too, and he assures them that this is the level on which God meets them and calls them to respond, by faith and love, to his word made flesh. All of this surpasses mere human understanding. This is precisely John's point: Christians are called to go beyond the framework and the limits of their sense experience, and to meet God on the level of faith, as he has presented himself to them in the person of Jesus, whose words are spirit and life, and whose works show his divinity.

John's message also contains a heavy emphasis on sacramentalism, which shows that he expects his followers to maintain a liturgical life-style, recognize his sacramental allusions and absorb the suggestions that he gives them on this level, even though they are often implicit.

In the light of all this, we may wonder what is the purpose of the Johannine Literature. The answer must be plural, since it has a number of purposes, although they converge in the Apostle's mind. John teaches in order to urge his followers to continue in their Christian faith, to avoid the things that threaten to weaken it, and to accept its consequences. We get the impression that John expects his Christians to undergo trials which probably will eventuate in martyrdom. He tries to equip them with the assurance that will enable them to accept this, and go to meet the Lord who has gone ahead to prepare a place for them in the Father's presence.

2

ON LIVING IN THE TRUTH:
The First Epistle of John

"Here, then, is the message
we have heard from him
and announce to you:
that God is light;
in him there is no darkness" (1 Jn 1:5).

Preliminary Reading

Read The First Epistle of John. Write down your comments and observations as you read.

Notice especially these thematic passages:

1:5-7   "God is light."

2:28-29 "Remain in him now."

4:7   "Let us love one another, for love is of God."

We can benefit greatly from starting our study of the Message of Saint John with the first of the three epistles which bears his name. It is shorter than the gospel, with five chapters rather than twenty-one. But the real reason for starting with the First Epistle, is that it is like an overture to the gospel, resuming in miniature, and in advance, the principal themes of the Johannine message that will recur in the Fourth Gospel, and again in the Book of Revelation, but to a lesser extent. Although the Epistle does not contain any narrative material, it does represent the mind and the style of the Beloved Disciple; the vocabulary and the level of theological insight which the Epistle represents are the same as those of the Fourth Gospel. So 1 Jn gives us a miniature course in the teaching, or in the spiritual doctrine, of the Beloved Disciple, based ultimately on his experience of Jesus. This is an excellent preparation for the fuller message of the Gospel According to John.

We can read the entire Epistle in a few minutes. It is lofty, uplifting, edifying. It is also challenging and demanding. There are some commentators who say that it is really a speech or a sermon, rather than an epistle, since it lacks the usual letter format, which would have the names of both sender and receivers at the beginning, as well as some kind of personal greeting or news, probably at the end. This may well be so. But it does not change the content. The author seems to be very anxious to have his friends, or followers, hold on to his teaching, and to help each other to hold and follow it, and to remain apart from those who do not. He maintains a fatherly attitude, calling them "my little children," or "my little ones" and "my beloved" (in the plural). These are clues which indicate that the teacher is elderly, and that he knows that he is respected by people who will receive his message.

The Central Theme

We usually like to figure out the plan or structure of a biblical book, in order to follow the development of its content or its message. But here we are somewhat stymied, because there doesn't seem to be any recognizable plan to the document. Instead of a logical order with introduction, body and conclusion, this document is more like a musical piece, that states a central theme, like a basic melody, and then proceeds to repeat it time after time, with variations of tone and key, but always maintaining the central theme.

So we try to find the central theme of 1 Jn. But as we read through the document, we come to the conclusion that the teacher knows what he wants to say, but the central point of his message is not a clearly defined thesis that we can analyze and discuss logically. Instead, it is an insight of faith, which adheres to a mystery, and witnesses to a person, rather than to a concept. There are both positive and negative elements in the message, so it seems that John's main thrust comes down to something like this: "hold the true and complete faith, and avoid anything or anyone that will compromise or weaken it!"

The central theme of John's message comes immediately in the opening four verses of the document; we proclaim to you what we have experienced, namely that eternal life has come to us; Jesus is eternal God in human form, and by holding our fellowship, or communion, with him, we have fellowship or communion with God, who is his Father and our Father, and we have it *now*.

This *now* is important, because it introduces us to a phrase which commentators use to describe a basic theme of Johannine theology, i.e. *realized eschatology*. This means that the final end time is *now*, not in the future. Instead of directing his disciples' attention to a promised future, John emphasizes that now is the time of salvation, because in the present time we have eternal life as a gift from God, if we relate to the full divine reality of Jesus on the level of faith. Because of this realized eschatology, John urges his followers to continue holding their faith as they have received it from him and his fellow apostles. If they do that, they already live as God's children, and they already possess the Holy Spirit, and this will bring them to separate themselves from "the world," i.e. from anything or anyone that is not animated by the same divine reality.

We said that there are negative elements in 1 John. These show up several times, as John tells his followers both what he means and what he does not mean, what they should do and what they should not do. We get the impression from this that John is disturbed and uncomfortable because of some dangerous tendencies among his Christian followers which are unacceptable to him. He warns them that "many anti-Christs have appeared . . . It was from our ranks that they took their leave" (2:18-19). He warns them further: "Have no love for the world . . . carnal allurements, enticements for the eye . . . the life of empty show" (2:15-16). And even the very last verse of the epistle ends the whole thing on a decidedly negative note (or perhaps it is a double negative). In any case, 5:21 says, "be on your guard against idols."

Now, it seems unlikely that John should find it necessary to warn his Christian followers in Ephesus against the dangers of the pagan idol cult. Not because it did not exist there, for it certainly did. But the Christians certainly knew by that time that idolatry was incompatible with their faith. So we suspect that the teacher means something else here. He probably is using this phrase as symbolic terminology, to warn them against the deception of settling for a merely sense-bound form of religion, since this would offer them less than the full truth that they can know on a supra-sensible level, by faith. If they believe in a Jesus who is less than divine, less God than the Father who sent him, they worship a mere idol.

This is why we say that John is witnessing here to a mystery, or to an insight of faith that he finds it difficult to define in conceptual terms. The teacher is uncomfortable because some members of his Ephesian church have been saying that Jesus is less than God, or less than really human. This weakens the content of the Church's faith, dilutes the wholeness of the mystery of Jesus' person, and draws an instinctive reaction from the teacher. Such an idea cannot go with the faith and witness of Christians. The whole reality that has come to men in the person of Jesus is the eternal reality of God who is truth and life and love. People who settle for less than that, are led not by divine faith, but by the short-range understanding of their human senses, and they fail to give God credit for what he has done.

This is the negative element that draws the teacher's warning; yet he is so graceful and delicate that he does not condemn or curse these defectors. But he warns his own friends to avoid them, to see that the anti-Christs do not see, and avoid the sense-bound idolatry of sense-bound religion, to love in faith and to walk in the truth, i.e. in the truth of the full mystery which God has graciously enthrusted to the Church.

Variations of the Central Theme

John varies the same central point three times, by presenting it under three different headings. The effect is somewhat like that of a kaleidoscope, which shows a constantly changing arrangement of the same pieces. The colors and the shapes are the same, but by shifting them around, the kaleidoscope shows them from different angles. Once he has made his central point, John now introduces the variations.

Light

The first variation presents the central message under the theme of *light*, which the teacher develops in thirty-three verses, from 1:5 through 2:27. Throughout this section he uses the technique of dualism, which will be another main feature of Johannine style. By contrasting light and darkness, he says both what is and what is not. In 1:5-7, he plays on the contrasting themes of light and darkness, and truth and lies. Hold the one, avoid the other. Then he applies the variation and the central theme, to his present situation, in 2:12-27, where he points out "the world," and the "anti-Christs" and "the liars" and defectors. "Anyone who denies that Jesus is the Christ, he is the anti-Christ, denying the Father and the Son" (2:22).

Fidelity

The second variation begins immediately in 2:28 and goes for thirty-three verses, to 4:6. John follows the same pattern again, but now the theme of the variation is *fidelity*: "Remain in him now, little ones" (2:28). The dualism shows up in the contrast between remaining in him, and following the way of sin, lawlessness and the devil. On the positive side, this means keeping God's commandment, which means believing in Jesus and loving one another (3:23). The present situation comes into view again in 4:1-6, as he now applies this variation to "false prophets;" these are the ones who fail to acknowledge Jesus Christ come in the flesh (4:2-3). This is a primitive exposition of what eventually will become the Church's dogma of the *Incarnation*. When he goes on to write the Fourth Gospel, this teacher will speak of the word which became flesh (Jn 1:14). Here he is reacting negatively and strongly against the very suggestion that the truth could conceivably be anything less than that.

Love

The third and final variation of the central theme goes for twenty-seven verses, from 4:6 to 5:12; the theme here is *love*. Interestingly, here the teacher introduces both the horizontal and vertical dimensions of love, just as he will do again in the Thirteenth chapter of the Fourth Gospel, when he speaks of Jesus' new commandment, to "love one another as I have loved you" (Jn 13:34-35). This variation is more practical and more ecclesial than the other two, since here the whole theme is really reduced to a concrete application of the message, which leads again to another illustration of Johannine dualism: As you hold the true faith, hold also by love to those who share this faith with you. Thus there are two kinds of people in John's world. This leads to the application of the third variation to the present crisis, as more clearly, perhaps, than before, John now sums up his teaching and his warning in 5:5-12: live by faith, stay with those who share the same pure faith, and avoid those who do not—these are men who reject God's own word and do not possess life, i.e. God's own life (5:10-12). This faith of ours conquers the world (5:4) i.e. it makes us live and perceive truth on a level which surpasses the limits of sense-knowledge.

The Johannine view of "the world" is quite negative, both here and also later on, in the Fourth Gospel. By this phrase the teacher means all those who are not led by faith and who consequently do not have a share in God's eternal life. We remember the Old Testament view of the world and of creation: "God saw that it was good" (Gn 1:4 etc.). However, here the difference is that when John speaks of "the world" in this context, he means those people who can see only the Jesus of the senses, the rejected prophet and the crucified criminal, without seeing by faith that he is the incarnation of eternal divinity, and the word made flesh. This is what John means by "the world" both here and in the Fourth Gospel (Jn 1:10 etc.). And he is against this kind of world, because Christians should be beyond its standards.

The Conclusion

Now that he has presented his central message and its three variations, John works toward a conclusion in 5:13-21. We see a remarkable similarity between 5:13 and the first conclusion of the Fourth Gospel (Jn 20:30-31): "I have written this to you to make you realize that you possess eternal life, you who believe in the name of the Son of God." This is the summary of the whole epistle, and of all of Johannine theology, for that matter. Christians must come to see the unsurpassable value of the treasure that they already have—they must keep it, because there is nothing on earth that will ever give them anything better. The danger is that their faith may weaken, and then they would fall away from the fullness of life which is theirs as God's gift.

John is also ecclesial in his conclusion, as he insists that his disciples must pray for each other. There is always hope for the brethren, as long as they have not fallen into the "deadly sin" (5:16-17). John does not specify what he means here by the "deadly sin," but it seems to be a reference to the one thing that he has been warning against throughout his message, i.e. apostasy, or heresy, or a combination of both.

The closing words of the message, 5:18-21, are another summary of the principal themes of the document; the characteristic Johannine dualism shows again, as John points out one way of life in contrast to another: the evil way of idols on the one hand, and, on the other, eternal life in Jesus who is the divine truth.

We leave our overview of 1 John with a final impression that John is really trying to communicate to his disciples an insight into what it means to be members of the Church. If they can only see this, then they should be so glad to keep this treasure pure and undiluted, that they will be on their guard zealously against any tendency to join those who have already compromised it and defected. The compromisers are apparently active and have confused some; the purpose of 1 John is to draw the line, close ranks and prevent the further spread of the confusion.

We have inherited twenty centuries of Christian faith and doctrine, including the Christological dogma of Jesus as true God and true man. For this reason we may find it difficult to appreciate the urgency which John feels and which is recognizable in both 1 John and the Fourth Gospel (as well as in Revelation). Perhaps we take the doctrine somewhat for granted nowadays, but the question had not been seriously raised in the earlier decades of the first Christian century, so it was not seriously contested. Now that some are saying, in the closing years of the same first century, that Jesus is not divine, or that he is less God than the eternal Father, or that he is not a man but a sort of unearthly super-spirit, the instinct of apostolic faith jumps to witness to the wholeness of the mystery that has come to the Church. The Church cannot be faithful to God, or to the identity that God has given it, if it allows any lessening or compromising its acceptance by faith of the full truth. If that would happen, it would mean that the Church is less than what God made it to be; we would only be God's servants. And this would fall short of the simple fact which John stresses—that God has bridged the abyss of his own eternity, and spoken a life-giving and creative word which makes us, like Jesus, his children.

Questions for Consideration and Reflection

1. Why do we study 1 John before we study the Fourth Gospel? Is 1 John an epistle?
2. What seems to be the essence of the message that the author seeks to present to his followers?
3. Is the plan or the structure of this document clearly recognizable? Is 1 John logical?
4. If we can anticipate the Fourth Gospel, what similarities or differences can we find between 1 John and the Fourth Gospel?
5. What seems to be the situation that prompted the author to produce this document?

6. Do the thematic passages indicated above (in the preliminary readings) adequately summarize the message of 1 John?

3

AN INTRODUCTORY OVERVIEW
OF THE FOURTH GOSPEL

"Eternal life is this:
to know you, the only true God,
and him whom you have sent, Jesus Christ" (Jn 17:3).

Preliminary Reading

Read through the entire Fourth Gospel; allow yourself about an hour to an hour and a half for this. Write down your comments and observations as you read. Try to build, in your mind's eye, a picture of the Fourth Gospel as a whole. Notice especially these parts of the Gospel:

1:1-18 The Prologue;
1:19-12:43 The Book of Signs;
12:37-43 Original Conclusion of the Book of Signs;
12:44-50 Appendix to the Book of Signs;
Chs. 13-20 The Book of Glory;
20:30-31 Original Ending of the Gospel;
Ch. 21 Appendix to the Book of Glory: the Risen Lord and his
       Disciples;
21:25 Conclusion of the Appendix and New Ending of the Gospel.

When we look at the Fourth Gospel, we usually find ourselves comparing it with the three Synoptic Gospels; this is natural enough, in terms of the similarity of the literary forms. However, in terms of the theological content, the real unity is between the Fourth Gospel and the other documents of the Johannine school, i.e. the three epistles and the Book of Revelation, or The Apocalypse. Nevertheless, when we undertake to compare the Fourth Gospel with the Synoptics, we see a striking combination of both similarities and differences. In all four, Jesus is central; the narrative pattern is basically the same, at least along the lines of his Public ministry, the Journey to Jerusalem, and then his Passion, Death and Burial, and then the Disciples' experience of the Risen Lord.

This shows us that all four of the evangelists follow and interpret the same basic apostolic teaching, but that John is remarkably independent, i.e. he is not independent of the apostolic faith, but he is independent of the Synoptic authors. After all, the Beloved Disciple had no need to draw from the writings of these earlier evangelists; he was able to draw upon his own personal recollections of his own experience. And this is exactly what he has done, and this is why his Gospel shows such originality. John teaches his followers his own understanding and interpretation of what he experienced and learned, many years before, even before many of his Ephesian disciples were born.

We have already seen that the fourth evangelist writes for several specific reasons, and these reasons are, for the most part, the same as the ones which led him to produce the first Johannine epistle; he gives his own reason at the end of the Gospel, in 20:30-31: "in order that you many believe . . . and have life in his name." So the Fourth Gospel is not written for prospective converts, or for non-believers, but rather to strengthen the belief of those who are already Christians.

From the beginning it is evident that the fourth evangelist writes from a perspective which is different from that of his Synoptic counterparts. Matthew speaks of Jesus as the descendant of Abraham and David; Mark shows him coming to receive baptism from John; Luke shows him born in the time of Ceasar Augustus. But John is less concrete than these, even though he is very definite and very specific. We see why, in classical Christian art, the symbol of the fourth evangelist is the eagle, since he soars here far beyond the context of earthly things, to speak of the beginning of all things, and the eternity and the life-and-being-giving Word of God, which became flesh and shared our humanity. "And," John says, "we saw his glory!" These are some of John's favorite theological themes— *glory* and *truth*; these words will recur often in the Gospel.

Immediately from the opening words of the Prologue (1:1-18) the evangelist draws the attention of his disciples beyond the framework of their own routine experience, and directs them to see the light which is the word of God and the life of men, shining in a darkness which is not strong enough to obscure it. This is another illustration of the dualism which we saw in 1 Jn—the contrast between light and darkness; creator and creation; eternity and history.

This is the way in which John introduces the central point of his Gospel: the thing that he has to say is utterly unimaginable, and unitelligible in terms of human understanding. Yet, for all of that, it is real; it has happened! This eternity, this very self-emission of divinity, has been here, for us to share and to know, for our sake, to bring us to himself.

All this came about when John was baptizing. Then along came Jesus who is the Lamb of God (John is the only New Testament author who uses this phrase to describe Jesus); and once Jesus appears, the Baptist recedes—and gladly, knowing that his work as the forerunner is done and over.

Thus the Prologue introduces the Gospel, and the Baptist introduces Jesus. All the lofty infinity of the Prologue now appears walking and talking, as Jesus gathers his disciples and begins his Public Ministry, bringing God's life to men.

Although there are some varying viewpoints, we are on good ground if we follow the opinion that the main lines of the Fourth Gospel are those of the Book of Signs (1:19-12:50) and the Book of Glory (chs. 13-20). These are flanked first of all by the Prologue (1:1-18), and then by the Redactor's Appendix (ch. 21).

The Book of Signs is a collection of scenes in which the evangelist presents Jesus performing a series of seven works of divine power, and, along with them, a great deal of discourse, both dialogue and monologue. This discourse is another special feature of John's style, and he uses it to present Jesus' words on the principal theological themes of the Gospel, and also to explain the meaning of the signs which they accompany.

The signs of the Fourth Gospel have a different theological meaning from the miracles of the Synoptic writings. These Johannine signs are not exorcisms in which Jesus brings the Kingdom of God and banishes evil power. Rather, John's point is that these are works by which Jesus manifests his glory (2:11), and which justify his disciples's belief in him—the disciples here being not only the original twelve, but Ephesian Christian followers as well.

As he goes on presenting these sign-scenes and the discourse material, the evangelist builds up a growing mood of tension. What happens is unimaginable and incredible, on two levels. First of all, it is unimaginable and incredible that God should show himself so openly and clearly, and then it is equally amazing that the leaders of his own people, the ones who should have known the Scriptures, should have been so blind as to miss what was as plain as day in front of their eyes. Nevertheless, this is exactly what has happened. Thus, the signs are life-giving manifestations of God's radiant presence—which is the same as Jesus' glory—his oneness with the Father. But the people who did not see by faith, tragically failed to recognize the reality that the signs presented to them.

In the Fourth Gospel Jesus is always divine, all-powerful and all-knowing, always in control of the situation. This shows us another feature of John's teaching, which is his technique of showing irony and misunderstanding. Even with the best of intentions, people never grasp the real level of meaning that Jesus intends. The reason for this is that they see only on a human level, whereas Jesus lives, works and speaks on the level of divinity. Each cameo scene of the Book of Signs shows this, that there is an abyss between the divine way of Jesus and the merely human way of men. Nicodemus; the woman at the well; the Jews at the pool; the crowds who eat the loaves; the leaders in the capital—they never get the message, not always because they lack goodwill, but always because they see only the human element, and miss the divine. By showing the irony of these people's obtuseness, John wants to challenge his Ephesian disciples to do better than these people did.

John sums up the message of the Book of Signs in 12:36-43, when he says that they simply refused to have faith. He quotes Isaiah's prophetic oracle containing the dualism of *seeing* and *blindness*. The real dualism that sums it all up comes in 12:43 "they preferred the praise of men to the glory of God." Human motives overcame divine faith. They were afraid that they might be expelled from the synagogue! The synagogue thinks that it has expelled the troublemaker. But who is the real loser? They have forfeited the gift of eternal life. This is the supreme irony, and the supreme tragedy that John wants his followers to avoid repeating.

If we read between the lines, we see that John is trying to draw a response from his disciples as he addresses this message to them. John has seen the Lord and his signs, and has heard the Lord's words, which he repeats here. His followers have not seen or heard. Yet they are Christians, because they have heard and follow the apostolic teaching. John knows that he must make his teaching vivid and limpid, in order to 'convince these disciples that this is the way to eternal life. This is why he uses the techniques of dualism and irony, to contrast the two ways—and he uses them well.

After the conclusion of the Book of Signs, we see a supplementary fragment (12:44-50). This fragment gives the words of Jesus and repeats several of the themes that we have seen so far. However, because this fragment is not organically related to the context, we conclude that a later redactor has added it here as an appendix to the Book of Signs, so that it would not be lost. The result is an inconsistency on the literary level, but it gives us some more of Jesus' words, none the less. Furthermore, it is another clue to the plurality of authors who have made a contribution to the final form of the Fourth Gospel.

The Book of Glory (chs. 13-20, plus, perhaps ch. 21) is John's way of showing his followers that Jesus took on his Passion with full control of the situation. It is the "hour" of his glorification; he is regal and free throughout, with royal purple, scepter, crown and title. This is irony, of course, and John specializes in it. Even Pontius Pilate cooperates without realizing it; he insists that the inscription over the cross must remain as it is—otherwise he would have to admit that he did not mean what he said.

The Book of Glory also includes the Last Supper Discourse in chs. 13-17. When we apply a literary analysis to these chapters, we find that they are composite, and this explains the element of repetition which is prominent here. Jesus gives his farewell and his parting words to the disciples whom he is leaving behind, as he goes to the glory of the Father's presence. Jesus is halfway between heaven and earth in these chapters, and he expects his disciples to join him there, where he is to be. John assures his Christian friends in Ephesus that the glorious Lord is waiting for them and that they should be ready to join him by taking the path of martyrdom, and that this will bring them to his and their Father's presence. In the meantime, which is the time of the Church—they will have the Holy Spirit as paraclete (advocate), comforter, counselor and teacher.

John presents the ecclesial element in Jesus' last words too. By washing their feet in ch. 13, Jesus gives the disciples an example of humility which they are to imitate by serving one another. He also gives them a new commandment—to love one another as he has loved them. This repeats, of course, the injunction which we saw in 1 Jn. It eventually becomes a hallmark of Christianity—"See how these Christians love one another!"

When we compare these last words of Jesus with the last discourse in the Synoptic Gospels (Mk 13; Mt 24-25; Lk 21), we see a major difference. The Synoptics show Jesus ready to depart as the Suffering Servant, who will come again as the vindicated and glorified Son of Man. John shows Jesus going away too, but he will come to the disciples by bringing them to his glorified self! The Fourth Evangelist does not promise a future kingdom of God on earth, or a glorious return of the Son of Man, because the glorious final end has already come. *This* is now the time of eternal life—the disciples share it *now* with Jesus, who brings it to them from the Father! Death will merely finalize and complete this union with him, to which he has already initiated them.

So the Last Supper Discourse leaves the disciples with a feeling of confidence and consolation; Jesus loves us, and we will see him again! This is what he said, and he is the truth, as well as the way and the life! All of this raises the disciples to a new level of life—the level of relating to the absent Lord on the level of faith—surpassing the level of sense-experience, and blurring the distinction which separates heaven from earth.

Jesus goes to his glory, enthroned on his cross, crowned and titled for all to see-if see they can, for the blind never will. His mother is there too, symbol of the church, woman of faith, as she was at Cana. She is given now into the care of the Beloved Disciple, who represents all his apostolic colleagues now, bereaved but not orphaned. Jesus sighs with satisfaction, "Now it is finished!" (19:30), and gives out his last breath, which is the Holy Spirit.

In the light of all this, the scenes of the Risen Lord do not show a break in the narrative, or a reversal of things. It is merely a continuation of what was there before. This is another difference between John's message and the earlier preaching of the kerygmatic witnesses and the Synoptic evangelists. Jesus was glorious before his death too, so that he now merely gives his disciples a glimpse of what he was before and still is. The thing that John stresses is not merely that Jesus is glorified after his death—for that is presupposed. The important thing is that only faith can relate to this glorified Lord, and only when and as the glorified Lord decides to show himself. The Beloved Disciple sees the empty tomb and believes; Peter, whose denial of the Lord has cost him dearly, comes off second best here. Mary of Magdala thinks only in terms of clinging to the flesh of the Risen Lord, and Jesus has to correct her. Her view is too dependent on sense and touch. Thomas makes a similar mistake, and the glorified Lord, rebukes him too. You don't have to see and touch to have faith—you only have to learn the truth from the witness of those who have seen and witnessed. It is sufficient to hear and to believe.

In conclusion of this brief overview, this is the message of the Beloved Disciple in his Gospel: we are God's children now, visited by his Son and taught by his Holy Spirit, who is the gift of the absent Lord. The world will never accept it because the world judges by its own merely human and sense-bound standards, not by God's. Jesus predicted this: "They will harry you as they have harried me" (15:20); "a time will come when anyone who puts you to death will claim to be serving God!" (16:2). What a confusion of values! This has apparently happened, and John wants to prepare his followers, so that they will be ready when it happens again, and accept it, cost what it may, and leave the victory to God.

Questions for Consideration and Reflection

1. How is the Gospel According to John similar to the three Synoptic Gospels?
2. What are two or three significant ways in which the Fourth Gospel differs from the Synoptic Gospels?
3. What are the dominant theological themes that the Fourth Evangelist repeats regularly?
4. What indications do we have that the Fourth Gospel is the "Spiritual Gospel" as distinguished from the three Synoptics, which are "material?"
5. Can we see the hand of more than one author in the final form of the Fourth Gospel?

4

THE NEW CREATION

"No one has ever seen God. The only Son, who is the same as God and is at the Father's side, he has made him known" (Jn 1:18).

Preliminary Reading

Read *John* 1:1-2:11. Write down your observations and comments as you read along. Notice especially these parts of the section:

1:1-18   The Prologue: From Heaven to Earth;
1:19-51   The Transition from John to Jesus;
2:1-11   The First Sign and the Response of the Disciples.

A. *From Heaven to Earth* (1:1-18)

The opening verses of the Fourth Gospel are so lyrical and rhythmic that they prepare us for the many similar passages which we will encounter throughout the Gospel, especially in the lengthy discourses of Jesus. Likewise, the themes of these opening verses are both a recall of the lofty terminology of 1 John, and also an introduction to the language-pattern of the Gospel itself.

We remember that the central theme of 1 John comes immediately in the opening words of the document. The same thing happens here; these opening verses present the essential content of the Fourth Gospel. What follows will merely flesh out what the evangelist has already said at the beginning. This is why we can call this passage the Prologue, or the Overture. Like the overture of an opera, it presents in miniature all the basic themes which will recur, on a larger scale, in the course of the work.

It is difficult to say for certain whether the evangelist has used a pre-existing hymn or poem (as some say) as the opening of his Gospel, or whether he has composed the whole thing himself precisely as the beginning of his Gospel. The style and tone are so similar to what will come in the later chapters, that this opening section is no less typically Johannine than the rest of the Gospel. It also shows the evangelist's deep insight into the biblical themes, and his ability to draw from them as he describes Jesus' work as the new creation.

We can easily understand why classical Christian artists use the prophetic image of the eagle as the symbol which best represents the fourth evangelist, since he soars upward and outward at the beginning of his Gospel, to draw his friends' attention to the lofty heights of heaven and eternity. This sets him apart from Matthew and Luke, who show in their Infancy Gospels the simple humanity of Jesus in his earthly origins. Mark begins his Gospel with the picture of Jesus as an adult, coming on the scene to receive baptism in the Jordan. In this the fourth evangelist agrees both with Mark and with the early apostolic preachers, whom we see represented in the speech of Peter in Acts 10:37 ff.: On the occasion of John's baptizing and preaching, Jesus appeared and began his ministry. But the Johannine genius makes its own special contribution by placing all of this within the larger context of heaven, eternity and creation. It reminds us of the cosmic view which characterizes the Jahwist and Priestly writers of Genesis; they also saw the relationship between God's saving action in the concrete events of their people's history, and the broader context of all creation, and the whole human family.

This is why we say that this evangelist is describing the new creation, and that this is his special way of interpreting the earthly work of Jesus. First, the great creation, then a passing mention of Moses, and of John the Baptist, and then, when the time is ripe, the Word becomes flesh, dwelling among men, to inaugurate the new creation, full of grace and truth.

Even the first scene of the Fourth Gospel builds upon the opening verses of Genesis. The first phrase in each of them is the same: "In the beginning . . ." (1:1). The evangelist in effect, is prephrasing the opening words of the Scripture! His first four verses draw from the first words of Genesis: God, in the vastness of his solitude, speaks his creative word, which comes from the timeless depths of his own being, and demands: "Let there be light!" (Gn 1:3). This creative word, as the self-expression of God, is a favorite theme of several Old Testament writers. The singer of Psalm 33:9 uses it: "He spoke, and it was created; he commanded, and there it stood!" This life-giving and being-giving word appears also in Ps 147:15-20, and 148:5-6.

The wisdom writers of Israel developed this image too, to give word-pictures of God's creative word as an emission of his wisdom, creating and ordering the universe. One of the most effective sages of the Old Testament was the composer of Proverbs 8, in which he shows Wisdom speaking its own autobiography: "Jahweh created me when his purpose first unfolded" etc. (Pr 8:22-31). Here Wisdom comes like a word from God's own inner self, and acts as his agent, helping him to fashion the universe. Sirach (ch. 24) presents a similar image of Wisdom coming from the mouth of God, like a creative word in the mist of primordial dawn, and coming to settle in Israel as the *Torah*, or Law, of Moses, God's great life-giving gift to his people. The Pseudo-Solomon who composed the Book of Wisdom describes Wisdom as a "breath of the power of God" and "an image of his goodness," so that the stage seems finally set for this "pure emanation of the glory of the Almighty" (Ws 7:24-26).

The Second Isaiah had the happy ability to combine the image of God's creative word with that of his plan for all of history. The very exuberant chapters of his oracles (Is 40-41) intertwine the image of the original creation with the new events of history; the exile will end, and God's people will be renewed as if by a new creation and a new Exodus (Is 41:17-20; also 44:24-28; 48:13-16; 55:10-11).

All of these themes and images serve the fourth evangelist, as he moves on to describe the momentous new creation which has occured. Now the same divine word has crossed the abyss of its own eternity to enter time and history, by coming to men and sharing their flesh. The life-giving true light came into the world which was his own domain, and "tented" among us! (Jn 1:14). And, just as he specializes in the dualism of light and darkness and of creator and creation, likewise the evangelist introduces here, for the first time, the irony which will be another principal feature of his literary and theological style. The supreme tragedy of all this is that "the world did not know him" and "his own did not accept him" (1:10-11). These are special Johannine words, "the world" and "know," which we have already seen in 1 John. "Knowing" means relating to God and/or to Jesus by faith, and "the world" means all who do not relate to Jesus by faith and therefore are imprisoned in their own sense-experience because they cannot recognize the divinity which presents itself to them.

But this tragic irony is offset and recedes to the background, as the amazing reality unfolds: "the Word was made flesh" (1:14). Nothing less, but indeed there is more: "We saw his glory . . . and of his fullness we have all received" (1:16). "Glory" in the Johannine vocabulary means the "glow" of God's recognizable presence, like the glow which hovered over the Ark of the Covenant in the desert (Ex 40:34-35), and which came to Solomon's Temple in Jerusalem (1 K 8:11). All of this has come to us, to make us God's children (1:12), and to give us what Moses and his Law could only foreshadow, i.e. the fullness of God's truth and favor (1:17).

This is the new creation, the work of the ony Son, who is the timeless Word, nearest to the Father's heart, sent by him to tell us about the Father (1:18). And John the Baptist is the bridge between the former creation and the new one. John is the witness, whose function was not to be the Messiah, but point people's attention to the One who was.

B. The First Week (1:19-2:11)

Throughout this next section the evangelist places a number of chronological clues, such as "the next day" (1:29, 43); "the following day" (1:35); "Three days later" (2:1). We know that the evangelist chooses his words carefully, so we are probably correct if we see that these days add up to a week, including the day of the Cana wedding sign. This is why we can trace the continuity of the evangelist's plan here, as he brings the attention of his friends back from eternity to time, and from heaven to history. The Baptist is the link, but he recedes gladly, once the preparatory stages are over and the time comes for the Word made flesh, to appear concretely in the person of Jesus.

There is a recognizable progresssion here, just as there is in the Prologue itself. First of all, John the Baptist appears witnessing to Jesus before the Jews (1:19-28); then he recognizes Jesus himself (1:29-34), and witnesses to him before his own disciples (1:35-42); in the last stages of the transition John does not appear at all, but the dialogue shows the new disciples going to Jesus (1:43-51). Once the transition is completed and the disciples have transferred their allegiance to Jesus, then Jesus "manifests his glory" in the Cana wedding sign. The disciples' response whereby they "believed in him" (2:11), becomes the prototypical act of discipleship, which Jesus will continue to demand throughout the remainder of the Gospel.

The fourth evangelist has "streamlined" the image of John the Baptist by eliminating a great deal of what the earlier evangelists have said about him. The earlier pictures which we have in the Synoptic Gospels, show John as a prophet and a moralizer. He calls for repentance and conversion, warning his countrymen to prepare themselves by symbolic washing, for the imminent judgment of God. His countrymen knew the Scriptures, and they were expecting a new prophet such as the one Moses had described in Dt 18:15-18, and like the returning Elijah of Malachi's oracle (Ml 4:5-6). But in the face of all the prominence and attention which he gets, there is something unexceptionably admirable about John. Not only in the more elaborate pictures of him which we have especially in the Gospels of Luke and Matthew, but even here in the more simplified Johannine rendering, John is humble and self-deprecating, as he forswears any title other than that of the herald's voice (Jn 1:23; Is 40:3).

It seems that even in the Fourth evangelist's day there were still followers of John the Baptist who were not yet followers of Jesus, just as there were in Paul's time a generation before (Ac 19:1-7). There may have been some great tension between them and the Christians of Ephesus, which led the evangelist to try so hard to show a complimentary picture of the Baptist which would do justice to the even greater importance of Jesus. Luke, of course, tries to do the same thing, by showing the careful Providence which God exercised in both of their births (Lk 1). Jesus eventually paid John the supreme compliment, calling him the greatest of all those who are born of women (Mt 11:11).

We can feel a touch of envy when we see the sharpness of John's insight; he recognizes not only who and what he is not, but also who, and what Jesus is, "the Lamb of God" (1:29) and "the Chosen One of God" or "the Son of God" (1:34). This latter title occurs earlier, in Peter's preaching (Ac 3:26) and frequently in the Synoptic Gospels. But the image of Jesus as the the Lamb of God is uniquely Johannine, and is one of the recognizable links that join the Fourth Gospel with the Book of Revelation, which uses the same image in the septet of the seals (Rv 4-6). Already here at the beginning of the Gospel, the evangelist foreshadows by this image, that Jesus is to save men by his blood and death at Passover time (Jn 13:1; 19:14, 31). The image is particularly apt, and shows the depth of John's insight into the symbolic value of Jesus' death, in the light of the biblical figures of the Passover lamb and the saving power of its blood (Ex 12:7), and the eating of its flesh (Ex 12:8). John also alludes here, implicitly, to the Second Isaiah's image of the Suffering Servant, who humbly submitted to death for the sake of others: ". . . he never opened his mouth, like a lamb that is led to the slaughter-house . . . While he was bearing the faults of many, and praying for sinners all the while" (Is 53:7-12). The "taking away" of the sins of the world suggests also an implicit allusion to the scapegoat of Lv 9:15, which the priests offered to God as a sacrifice of reparation, piling onto it all their sins.

The Disciples

Now it is time for the disciples to appear, and the Baptist moves them gently away from himself to Jesus, who has appeared for the first time, baptized now and accompanied by the Holy Spirit. We may suspect that the evangelist had a trace of a smile on his face, as he told of these first disciples, and of their confusion and puzzlement. They accept the Baptist's direction, and leave him to follow Jesus. But they seem to have not the slightest idea of what to do. Jesus shows himself to be in command of the situation as he turns and surprises them by his obvious question. But he saves them from embarrassment by his graciousness and hospitality. Even though it is difficult, if it is possible at all, to reconcile this scene with the call of the disciples in the Synoptics, it shows the kind of nuance and knowing insight, that suggest an eyewitness, so that the Beloved Disciple himself may well have been one of these anonymous first disciples.

In the four incidents which he describes here, the one thing that the evangelist holds constant is the superiority of Jesus. He immediately moves forward to center stage, which the Baptist readily relinquishes. Jesus accepts the homage of the anonymous ex-disciples of John. He justifies the confidence of Andrew, who calls him nothing less than the Messiah, and he confers upon Simon the name by which he will be known through the coming centuries; he surprises Nathanael by showing him that, even without realizing it, Nathanael had been the object of his interest, and that there are more surprises yet to come. In the next scene Jesus will work the first sign, and justify thereby their faith in him.

All four of these scenes tantalize us by the thinness of detail which the evangelist gives. He seems to know well enough what he wants to say, and he has the scenes clearly in his own memory. Indeed, they appear to be, as we said, the Apostle's own reminiscences. But we can only wish that he had been more generous in describing these scenes! He says enough to remind himself of the incidents, but he appears to leave unmentioned some more details, and takes it for granted that his readers should know them too! We can only wish that we were there in Ephesus, to ask the Apostle to fill in these pictures for us—or, even better, we can wish that we had been there when Jesus first came upon the scene, in that first week of the new creation!

It is remarkable that already at the end of this first chapter, Jesus has acquired a long list of titles. He is the *Word; God; Light; Life of Men; Only Son; Word made flesh; the One nearest to the Father's Heart; the Lamb; God's Chosen One; Rabbi/Teacher; Messiah/Christ; Son of God; King of Israel; Son of Man.* As the chapter closes, Jesus suggests another designation for himself by recalling the image of Jacob's ladder (Gn 28:12) and the saying which accompanies it: "Truly, the Lord is in this spot, although I did not know it! . . . This is nothing else but an abode of God, and that is the gateway to heaven!" In this cryptic way Jesus tells Nathanael that, although the disciples may not realize it, they are now dealing with the one who is the link between man and God.

Cana

Sometimes, as we read and re-read this passage, we get the impression that there are a number of things that the evangelist has left unsaid. True enough, this is the first of the signs, as he says in 2:11. But the conversation between Jesus and his mother is puzzling: Jesus tells her that it is not yet time, and then he works the miracle anyway! And there is no indication at all of the reaction of the people who benefitted most from Jesus' act, i.e. of the bride and groom, much less of the other guests at the wedding. For all of these reasons, as we said above, the evangelist seems to know clearly what he means to say, but we can only wish that he would have given more details! We are compelled to conjecture, as we try to figure out what he means to suggest, in his very highly nuanced way.

We get some clues from the context. We have already noted that 2:1 makes this the last of a series of events, which come together as the first week of the new creation. Also, 2:1 makes this the first of a series of signs, which will come to a conclusion in 12:37-43. The disciples appear at the beginning of the scene and again at the end. Apparently, the transition from John to Jesus is completed, and now the stage is set to show the special relationship that must exist between Jesus and those whom he has made his disciples.

One respectable opinion holds that this was originally a "hidden life" story, like that of Jesus lost and found in the Temple, and growing in age and favor with God and men (Lk 2:41-52), which the evangelist had placed here to show the beginning of Jesus' Public Ministry. Another explanation is that the Apostle was present at the wedding, as one of the newly-recruited disciples (2:2), and that he reminisces here, although his recollections are blurred as they are transmitted more than half a century after the event. Nevertheless, the main lines come through, and we find that we have no choice but to content ourselves with these.

It is the first appearance of "the mother of Jesus" in the Fourth Gospel. She appears only once more, at Calvary (19:25-27). Jesus accedes to her request in spite of the fact that his "hour" has not come (2:5). This "hour" is another special word of the Johannine vocabulary, meaning the time at which Jesus is to be glorified and return to the Father. When Mary reappears at Calvary, it is the "hour" (13:1). Both at Cana and at Calvary she is the favored one; both at Cana and at Calvary she represents those for whom Jesus has come, i.e. the people of faith, who will eventually emerge as the Church. Some say that the water of Cana represents baptism, and the wine represents the eucharist, but this is probably reading into the text something which the evangelist did not intend. However, it is credible that he uses the incident to show that Jesus inagurates the new age, or the new creation, symbolized by the good new wine, in place of the former dispensation of the old Israel, represented by the water. And the ones to whom Jesus shows his glory by this sign, are the disciples, in order that he may demand and justify their belief in him (2:11). This explains the irony of the contrast between the reaction of the steward, who shows by his response that he has not the slightest understanding of what has happened, and the disciples, who, without speaking, "believed in him" (2:11). The "glory" that Jesus mainfests here is the same as the glory that "we saw" in 1:14, i.e. a "glowing" manifestation of God's presence. In the Old Testament this "glory" was visible in the form of a cloud or a fire; now, in the new creation, it is visible in the person of Jesus, because of the signs.

Conclusion

The new creation is now in effect. Jesus, with his disciples, who believe in him, is now in center stage. The themes which the evangelist introduces in the Prologue will now work themselves out in the succeeding chapters. The first of the signs inaugurates a series of them, which will come on now like a succession of theophanies, seven in all, showing Jesus' divine power and glory, and demanding a response of divine faith—nothing less will do.

Questions for Consideration and Reflection

1. Does the terminology of First John prepare us well to receive the message of the Fourth Gospel? Is the terminology of the Prologue a good preparation for that of the rest of the Gospel?
2. Does the evangelist show the Old Testament sources of his terminology?
3. In the "opening days" (1:19-51) does the evangelist show clear clues to the divinity of Jesus?
4. What is the role of Mary at Cana? What is the point of the whole Cana wedding incident?
5. Which titles of Jesus are peculiar to this chapter?

5

THE FIRST PILGRIMAGE

"I solemnly assure you, no one can see the reign of God
unless he is begotten from above" (Jn 3:3).

Preliminary Reading

Read Jn 2:12-4:54, writing down your observations and comments as you read. Notice especially these features:

2:12-25   The two temples;
3:1-12   The incomprehension of Nicodemus;
3:13-36 The contrasting of themes; the *water* theme;
4:1-42   The response which Jesus gets from non-Jews;
4:43-54 The second Cana sign.

The fourth evangelist makes the various Jewish feasts the background for the whole remainder of his Gospel. He shows Jesus now presenting himself and his teaching on the occasion of the Passover festival, which he mentions in 2:13. Later he will mention a Sabbath, another Passover, the feasts of Tabernacles and of Dedication, and then the great Passover which forms the back drop for Jesus' death and resurrection.

This is a way of making the point that Jesus and what he has to offer, are better than what the old Judaism and its old observances had to offer. The new creation which came in the first section of the Gospel, is now in effect, and in this next section, it goes on to become new life. Jesus now offers this new life not only to the limited circle of his disciples, but to "the Jews," who fail to respond, and to the Samaritans, the legendary outsiders of Israel, who, surprisingly, are thrilled and grateful as they respond to Jesus' offer with faith and goodwill. As he returns home to Galilee after his Passover pilgrimage to Jerusalem, Jesus works the second sign, but even here the evangelist shows that the Samaritans look better, bacause they believe on the word of Jesus, without demanding any signs.

A. The New Temple (2:12-25)

The Passover was the principal feast of the Jewish year, and the Temple in Jerusalem was the principal holy place of Israel. Jesus was not the only one who made the traditional pilgrimage, but we can be sure that the people who made it that year saw something that they had not expected to see! We can also wonder, though, how many of them understood the message that came to them. Even though the Temple Cleansing is not, strictly speaking, a miracle story, nevertheless the evangelist seems to offer it as one of the special challenges that Jesus presented to his people, but that they failed to recognize the point of it all.

We can see that the evangelist describes the incident in the light of the known reality of Jesus' resurrection, since he alludes to it in the dialogue between Jesus and "the Jews." The overriding theological significance of the event is more important in the evangelist's mind than the actual time of its occurrence, as we see from the fact that he places it first in the Public Ministry, in contrast to all three Synoptics, who place it at the end of the Public Ministry sections of their Gospels.

The Johannine message comes through clearly. Now that he has inaugurated the new creation and justified his disciples' faith in himself, Jesus goes to the center of Judaism and challenges his own people to choose between everything that the Temple represents, and the mystery of his own person. Even though the Synoptic evangelists describe the incident too, the special Johannine contribution comes in the brief but terse dialogue between Jesus and his unbelieving countrymen, whom the fourth evangelist consistently describes as "the Jews." Jesus turns the whole incident into a mysterious allusion to his own body, which will be raised up in three days. John may have been one of the disciples present at this confrontation, although he understood it only later, after he had experienced the presence of the Risen Lord. This is why the evangelist can say, "Only after he had been raised from the dead did the disciples remember all this . . ." (Jn 2:22). "The scripture" which the evangelist mentions may be a combination of "raising up" and "third day" texts such as Ps 16:10 and Ho 6:2-3, as well as Jonah 2:1, to which Jesus himself alludes in Mt 12:40.

As Jesus' Public Ministry opens, there is an element of *chiaroscuro*—the light of resurrection and new life, mingled with the darkness of his own people's unfaith, and of his coming death, which the evangelist anticipates already at this early stage, just as he did more cryptically in the Baptist's description of Jesus as the Lamb of God (Jn 1:29-36). We do not get the account of everything that Jesus did during this visit to Jerusalem, but the evangelist does indicate that Jesus did more (2:22; 4:45). Even so, this one incident must suffice to show that Jesus has made his point, but that the response has been less than what it should have been. The concluding verses of the chapter (2:22-25), and the dialogue between Jesus and Nicodemus (ch. 3), summarize the lack of faith-rapport which characterizes Judaism's response to God's gift offered in the Word made flesh.

B. The New Birth (3:1-12)

Along with several other tragic characters in the Gospels, Nicodemus remains for all time unrehabilitated as a man who meant well but never really succeeded. At his first appearance in the Gospel he is courteous (3:2); at his second appearance he is scrupulously honest and just (7:50-51), and at his third and last appearance he is helpful, sympathetic and generous (19:30). But, for all of that, he never comes to the one thing that matters, which is accepting Jesus on the level of faith. In this Nicodemus remains forever uncomprehending and pathetic along with his countrymen of the preceding incident. And, by the same token, he is tragically—almost comically—outpaced by the unaffected simplicity of the Samaritan woman of the next chapter, who is so flattered by the Messiah's gift of himself, that she leads her neighbors to faith.

Both the Nicodemus chapter (ch. 3) and the Samaritan chapter (ch. 4), are still within the Passover atmosphere of Jesus' first visit to Jerusalem, and both show the fourth evangelist's masterful use of irony to show people's failure to understand Jesus. There is also the constant intertwining of the themes of *water* and *life*, as well as a flashback to the figure of John the Baptist (3:22 ff.), as the evangelist's mind clicks into focus at the baptismal suggestion that comes through implicitly from Jesus' fruitless discussion with the uncomprehending councillor.

How tragic it is that this prestigious intellectual had to hide his interest in Jesus under the cloak of nocturnal secrecy (3:2). And yet, this fear of human respect is not his only failure. It is even more tragic that he misses the subtle point of Jesus' response, which could have been like a key for him, unlocking the mystery of the signs (3:3). But Nicodemus made the fatal mistake which the evangelist depicts in high relief: he remained imprisoned on the level of sense-understanding, while Jesus spoke of the level of spiritual reality, and never the twain do meet! The result is that there is such an abyss between them that they never reach a genuine mutual understanding.

What Jesus offers is a spiritual lesson that is no less real than the unseen wind. But for this unimaginative leader, who should be steeped in spiritual insight, the prospects of being begotten from above, or of being begotten of water and Spirit, make little sense. Sad that such a respectful and well-intentioned leader should be so obtuse as to miss what is so obvious to faith. Jesus now rebukes him with what may be the most devastating retort in any of the Gospels, and from here on embarrassed councillor fades out of the picture with nothing more to say or offer. The Johannine dualism of flesh and spirit, and of earth and heaven, summarizes the unfortunate contrast of the two mindsets (3:10-12).

C. The Monologue (3:12-21; 31-36)

A number of times the fourth evangelist starts out presenting a dialogue, as he does here, but then his own mind seems to wander somewhat, so that he rambles on with related themes, but we are at a loss to be sure where the dialogue ends and a monologue supervenes. After 3:12 there is no more address to "you" and so we can follow the evangelist's own mind here, as it shifts to a monologue on the dualism of *heaven* and *earth; up* and *down; save* and *condemn; light* and *darkness; truth* and *false.* Even so, we are no less reduced to conjecture as to whether the speaker of the monologue is Jesus himself (3:13-21), or the evangelist. In the latter section of the chapter, the Baptist reappears, briefly, and then the monologue resumes again in 3:31-36. This seems to be the evangelist's rambling way of highlighting Jesus' challenge to the outmoded *Torah* lore and sense-bound myopia that kept Nicodemus and his fellow Jews from recognizing the greater gift that offered itself to them. If only they had been able to see and speak the things of the Spirit which came to them in the person of Jesus and in his mysterious words, they could have been "begotten from above," or, as some translators prefer to have it, if perhaps less precisely, "born again."

The evangelist shows again that he sees all of this by hindsight, in the light of the mystery of the Risen Lord. For his play on "up/down" refers not only to the heaven-to-earth movement of the *Word made flesh* which he described in his Prologue, but also to the "down/up" Lord, crucified, resurrected and ascended, who is the object of Christians' faith (3:14). This throws light also on Jesus' insistence on being begotten of both water and Spirit (3:5), since the Spirit who is given in the birth-water of baptism, is the Spirit of the Risen Lord. And the life-giving Spirit comes from the one who has been "lifted up." The almost-forgotten figure of the brazen serpent might have remained buried forever in Old Testament folklore, if the Johannine mind had not drawn it out as a type of the lifted-up Lord's power to defeat death by giving men life. Even the "must" of 3:14b shows that all of this is no accident, but, in retrospect, and especially in the clear light that comes with the distance of reflective years, it is evident that it was all planned by God, whose Word this is.

All of this is gift (3:16), as the teacher has already said in 1 Jn 4:9-10. And in the giving there is a getting, since God gave his Son to death (as Paul told the Romans also, in Rm 8:32), in order to ransom "whoever believes in him." There would have been no alternative to this death for men, if there had been no giving by God, and for those who have no faith, there can be no getting of this gift. Tragically, this is not promising for Nicodemus' people, since the evangelist cannot offer them the assurance of life and light that he can guarantee to his fellow Christians. "Darkness" and "judgment" are hard words; but the evangelist has nothing else to offer to those who remain on the other side of the invisible barrier. All of this is remarkably similar to the message which this same teacher presented earlier in the first Johannine epistle (1 Jn 3:1-4:6).

God's plan is to transform the world by giving men a share in his own life, through faith in Jesus. This means that by relating to God's gift in this way, we have heaven on earth, and we have it *now*! Another special feature of the Johannine literature, is the emphasis on the present time and the present world. Our salvation is now and our sharing in God's life is not something in the future that we can only await! Johannine theology does not hold out the prospect of waiting for an eventual return of Jesus, as both Paul and the Synoptics do; rather, John's message is that the future is already here, in an earthly life divinized by faith! This is what Jesus offered in his earthly life. When he finished his earthly mission, death was for him merely a sort of doorway through which he passed, from earth and time to the eternity of the Father's presence. And for these who "act in truth" and "come into the light" the same thing happens. Christians live God's life, given to them by the Word made flesh, and they live it now (3:3-6).

The Baptizer (3:22-30)

These contrasting themes of the monologue remind the evangelist again of the Baptist's witness to Jesus. The significance of water and the Jewish purification rites reminds him again of the baptizing ministries of both John, and Jesus and his disciples. But he uses this last picture of John to strengthen the picture of Jesus. Just as Jesus replaces John the Baptist, the Temple and its observances, and Nicodemus' sense-bound religion as well, so too the new baptism of Christians replaces the ineffective purification rites of Israel (3:25). The evangelist's own teaching causes him to recall John here, somewhat illogically, since John has already witnessed to Jesus (1:19-37). But this shows the key to this Gospel's language-pattern: it is spiritual insight which suggests basic themes in narrative form. Precision of time and place takes second place here, as the themes of *water-life* and the contrast between the old way and the new life, come to the fore. The Baptist's last words in 3:30 could apply not only to himself, but also to all the Israelite institutions which the evangelist presents in this section of his Gospel.

D. The New Life (4:1-42)

The scene shifts now to Samaria, halfway, approximately, between Jerusalem and Nazareth. But the geographical factor is quite secondary for the evangelist, whereas he is very much interested in the fact that in comparison to "the Jews" at the Temple and to the sophisticated but uncomprehending Nicodemus, Jesus gets along much better with not only the Samaritans, who were like the "black sheep" of Israel, but with a woman at that (4:9, 27). The *water* theme with its subtle hint of baptism, carries over from the preceding chapter. But with what a difference! Instead of spiritual blindness by night, here we have spiritual awakening in the broad light of midday

(4:6). Jesus here presents himself as the source of living water, and thereby claims that he has more to offer than even Jacob and Joseph, the revered patriarchs of Israel (4:5). There is another challenge here too, as Jesus dismisses both the Jerusalem Temple and the rival Samaritan shrine on Mount Gerizim (4:19-24), in order to insist that both these centers are now obsolete, since God now calls upon men to worship him spiritually, as he really is (4:23-24), apart from national or sectional loyalties.

We usually do not think of humor in the Scriptures, in general, or in the Gospels in particular, but the evangelist must have gotten a good laugh from his disciples, as he described the respectful but ironic obtuseness of the woman's response to Jesus' offer of living water (4:11-12)! Again we see a sample of Johannine irony, perhaps at its best here! And once is not all! She misunderstands yet a second time (4:15), but now, instead of being preoccupied by Jesus' lack of a bucket, she is thrilled at the prospect of having an endless supply of water within herself! Instead of having an insight into the prospect of sharing God's eternal life, she can see no further than her daily trek to the well (4:15).

With all of her moral weakness and sense-bound understanding, she is honest and respectful; she recognizes Jesus as a prophet (4:19). This is something, but how greatly this falls short of the total reality! Yet, when Jesus tells her plainly that he is no less than the promised Messiah (4:26), she accepts the revelation and becomes his agent, impressed by his superhuman knowledge of her life-history (4:17).

The evangelist has not exhausted his irony and humor yet; even Jesus' own disciples come in for a touch of his good-natured needling here, as he shows them completely unable to grasp Jesus' intention. They are surprised that Jesus should be talking to a woman, but they miss entirely the higher level of Jesus' metaphor on food and harvest (4:34-48). Jesus is hungry, but not for earthly food! The thing that he eagerly craves, is to carry out the mission that the Father has entrusted to him, and harvest a real bumper crop of believers! The Samaritans are to be his harvest! The time has come! Israel has missed its chance, and now the outsiders are to have theirs. This message could hardly be lost on John's Ephesian Christians, who would be glad to have this explanation of how and why the Church has become so rapidly more gentile than Jewish. The answer is evident in the contrast between the sterile orthodoxy represented by Nicodemus, and the sinful but grateful faith of this half-breed harlot, and of her enthusiastic countrymen, who demand no signs but believe on the basis of her word and of his (4:41-42). Jesus is now not only the King of Israel (1:49), but, as the Samaritans see, he is "the Savior of the world" (4:42). This is the kind of faith that Jesus wants, and the kind that the evangelist is trying to elicit! This is the kind of faith that the Ephesian church needs to have, the kind that Thomas had to learn (Jn 20:29), since it responds to God without demanding evidence for the senses.

E. Back in Galilee; Another Sign (4:43-54)

The Passover pilgrimage ends as Jesus comes back home to Galilee. Oddly enough, there seems to be a tension between the welcome that he gets because of his reputation as a wonder-worker (4:45), and the eventual outcome of his Galilean ministry as a whole, which the evangelist summarizes in 4:44. Ultimately, of course, neither Galilee nor Jerusalem gets credit for responding to Jesus with true divine faith, as the evangelist says in 12:37 ff.

The fourth evangelist is the only one who places the healing of the boy in the village of Cana, although both Matthew (ch. 8) and Luke (ch. 7) preserve what appear to be parallel accounts of the same incident. The variations in the three renderings are understandable in the light of both the flexibility of oral tradition, and the independence of John's reminiscences. It is not terribly important whether it was a centurion's servant in Capernaum, or a "royal official's son" in Cana. But for the Johannine rendering there is no hint here of the universalism which characterizes the Lukan and Matthean accounts; here it is simply another sign, showing now publicly the same power that the first sign manifested privately to the disciples (2:11).

The royal official was apparently an employee of Herod Antipas, who was a son of Herod the Great and the killer of John the Baptist (Mk 6), as well as the one who abused Jesus during his Passion (Lk 22). Jesus did not like this Herod (Lk 13:32-33), but this did not keep him from responding to the plea for life (4:49). After speaking so much about it, he now will show a sample of his power to give it.

Even so, Jesus seems impatient here, at a faith that cannot live without depending on signs. The Samaritans did better (4:41-42)! Signs support faith; they cannot cause it. The kind of faith that Jesus demands, does not need signs (4:50), but the signs that he offers are wasted when people do not accept them in faith. The official's virtue is his faith; his weakness is his need for a sign. His mistake is like that of Thomas (20:29).

Summary

As the rhythm of the Fourth Gospel advances, the mystery unfolds; the new creation has come as new life, but there are tragedies of failure as well as notes of success. The evangelist varies the vocabulary sometimes, speaking of faith, belief, trust. But, under any label, some respond correctly and some do not. Johannine dualism brings a tremendous tension, and makes a tremendous demand. It was difficult enough for those who saw and heard Jesus, to overcome their preconceptions and accept the truth that presented itself to them; it is even more difficult for John's Christians now, since they have not the signs, but the Apostle's word, and its call for a demanding faith, in an absent Lord.

Questions for Consideration and Reflection

1. What is the point of the Temple Cleansing in 2:12 ff.? How does the Johannine rendering of the scene compare with the corresponding scenes in the Synoptic Gospels?
2. How do the images of Nicodemus and the Samaritan woman come across?
3. How does the evangelist develop the symbolism of the *water* theme? Does he speak here of sacramental baptism?
4. Does the evangelist give clues to show that he sees these incidents in the light of the mystery of Easter?

5. Do we see many examples of irony in these chapters?
6. How does the evangelist show the disciples responding to Jesus?

6

SABBATH LIFE AND PASSOVER BREAD

"Jesus said to them, 'I am the bread of life; he who comes to me shall not hunger, and he who believes in me shall never thirst' " (Jn 6:35).

Preliminary Reading

Read Jn chs. 5-6. As you read these chapters, jot down whatever observations or comments come to your mind. Notice especially these points:
1. The feast-days in the background, and the connection which the evangelist establishes between them and the signs;
2. The themes of Johannine theology which are especially prominent in these chapters;
3. The different reactions that greet Jesus and the signs.

As the Fourth Gospel unfolds, some of the basic lines which have been evident from the opening verses continue to appear, and at the same time there are several new features which the evangelist introduces here, and which will remain through to the end of the Gospel. Jesus is still the Word made flesh and the Son of Man who challenges people to relate to him by faith. Some do, but others fail to understand and believe. He continues to present himself against the background of Israel's principal feasts and institutions, but, in each instance, somehow, he is also above them. But now, for the first time in the Fourth Gospel, what was incomprehension and resentment on the part of "the Jews" grows here to be nothing less than persecution and a decision to destroy him. More and more the Twelve emerge as the ones who respond to Jesus by faith, although they are never free of their human limitations.

In both of these chapters we see a certain uniformity of the evangelist's pattern. Each chapter consists basically of a sign plus discourse (in ch. 6 there are two signs); in the discourse Jesus explains the meaning of the signs, and asserts the unique authority which he has because of his unique relationship with the Father. He asserts his divinity and demands faith in himself as the only thing that will enable people to understand him or to receive what he has to offer. He asserts that he is superior to the Jewish institutions, but this only enrages his enemies and sets their tragic unfaith in high relief. Human nature, by itself, is inadequate to the challenge that Jesus presents. This makes the true meaning of discipleship, and its demands, starkly evident.

A. *The Man on the Mat (ch. 5)*

Tourists and pilgrims who visit Jerusalem nowadays can see the pool which was the setting of this sign. Near the Gate of St. Stephen, within the grounds of what is now the church of St. Anne, archaeologists have been notably successful in excavating and bringing to light this pool with its porticoes, and the layout of the area corresponds remarkably with the picture which the evangelist gives at the beginning of this chapter. Perhaps the water had some thermal or mineral properties that the ancient people understood as miraculous healing power. But the thing that the evangelist wants to present is the piety which Jesus himself shows in going to Jerusalem for the feast, while at the same time he acts on his own initiative in healing the crippled man on the Sabbath. More and more the irony builds up, until it becomes absurdity, as "the Jews" upbraid the healed man for such a simple thing as carrying his bedroll on the holy day, missing entirely the undeniable miracle that has occurred in front of their eyes! The healed man has no cause to defend; he does not even know who his benefactor is, until Jesus reappears—again on his own initiative—and invites him to advance to the new life which is available to him, in faith.

All the tragedies of the incident come together (5:16-18). The leaders criticize the healed man because God has touched his life in a way that does not fit into their limited view of religion. The sharpness which they showed toward Jesus at the Temple Cleansing (2:12-25), now advances to become nothing less than a persecution of him because he challenges their sabbath formalism. This persecution advances even further when Jesus dares to claim divine authority for what he does. God continues his providence even on the Sabbath, giving life and sustaining his people; and what the Father does, Jesus does too. This is too much for the leaders, and this brings them to the decision that Jesus must be eliminated. Of course, the supreme irony of all is that they have correctly understood what Jesus has claimed, for otherwise they would have been able to ignore him. But, what Jesus says and does, cannot fit with what they think and expect of God. It must be his way, or theirs.

The Discourse (5:19-47)

What Jesus responded briefly to the leaders in 5:17, he now expands into the first of the major Johannine discourses. We will become accustomed to this feature of the Fourth Gospel, as we see the other discourses in the coming chapters. In these discourses the evangelist reproduces sayings of Jesus in such a way that they emphasize the principal themes of his teaching, and explain the signs which he performs.

5:19-30   If Jesus were acting on his own power and authority, he would be great enough. But he is even greater than that, because he is the Son and he is doing only what the Father does. He has already spoken of God as his Father, but there he develops this explanation so fully that we can only marvel at the depth of the intimacy which he has with the Father. We can see here also the fruit of the Beloved Disciple's reflective pondering of the depth of meaning which attaches to Jesus' words, as he remembers them from many years before. We can see that John has recognized in Jesus the power which the Scriptures ascribe to God, especially that of giving life. This was one of the evangelist's first statements, back in the Prologue, and now it reappears on Jesus' own lips! This supreme power over life Jesus has already shown in a gradual way, by healing first the royal official's son (Jn 4), and now the crippled man; he will show it again when he heals the blind man (Jn 9) and calls Lazarus from his tomb (Jn 11), and, supremely, when he presents his Risen self to his still-uncomprehending disciples (Jn 20). John is also anxious here to encourage his Christian friends to preserve in their faith even in the face of possible martyrdom, confident that the Lord will raise them to new life by his power which the Father has shared with him. The future-orientation of Jesus' work show up also in his use of the themes of the *Son of Man* and of *judging*, which he claims also as the Father's commission to him (5:22). Jesus draws here from the apocalyptic imagery of Daniel 7, in which the prophetic visionary of the Old Testament sees the Son of Man victorious over all his former oppressors, and empowered by God to be the final arbiter of their destiny. This image is common enough in the Synoptic Gospels, but Jesus appears to use it here not so much to refer to his own vindication, but rather to the divine authorization which backs up his work. He seems also to be giving a subtle hint of the sign that he will perform soon, when he restores Lazarus to his mourning sisters (Jn 11:43).

5:31-40   This is really not a conversation between Jesus and his critics, since they disappear quite early in the chapter. But even so, there is a crescendo in this monologue, as Jesus builds up his rebuke of the self-righteous orthodoxy of those who resist him precisely on what they claim to be religious grounds. If they really wanted to serve God, they would recognize the signs and witnesses which God gives them! Jesus cites now four witnesses to himself that should be more than sufficient to convince anyone with good will. First of all there is the witness of John the Baptist, who publicly declared for Jesus. Like it or not, John could have had a great following for himself, but he never claimed to be more than the one sent by God to prepare people's attention for the appearance of Jesus. Secondly, how can they be so willfully blind as to refuse to see the plain reality of the signs which Jesus has performed? We do not know how many signs there were: the evangelist has given three so far, with four more to come, but he says that there were more (2:23; 4:45; 20:30; 21:25). How many do they need? If they had faith, one would be more than enough. Anyone not mired in the sense-bound blindness of callous unfaith, would spontaneously recognize the witness of Jesus' mighty works. The interior testimony of faith would speak in their hearts if they had truly divine religion, and this would be the Father's witness to Jesus, which they would recognize and follow. The fourth witness to Jesus is Moses, who wrote (Dt 18:15-18) that a prophet would come. Since they claim to follow the teachings of Moses and to be loyal to the Scriptures, how can they miss this testimony? A damning rebuke indeed that Jesus levels at them—that they simply refuse to accept the gift that God offers them and advance to the fullness of their life-potential.

5:41-47   The situation is like the positive and negative elements of a photograph. Because they reject the positive witnesses who could teach them the truth, these leaders show only negative qualities. These unbelieving critics (whom the fourth evangelist consistently calls "the Jews") are governed by merely human or earth-bound motives. They may be interested in religion, but they do not recognize God where he chooses to show himself! This short-sightedness that fails to see the fullness of Jesus' person was also the danger that we saw in the first Johannine epistle (1 Jn 2:22-23).

The evangelist now repeats the contrast between a merely human view of Jesus and a view of him which is guided by God's own love; hearts and eyes which are guided this way, see and love God as he comes to them in the person of Jesus, and in his words and works. For the chosen people the ultimate tragedy is that they miss the fulfillment of their own heritage, since, if they had really followed the testimony of Moses, they would see it fulfilled in Jesus. But the great lesson of all this is that there are none so blind as those who will not see.

Jesus is sharp here; yet we could hardly expect him to be on pleasant terms with such stubborn hostility. The healed cripple and the Sabbath have faded into the background; so have the critics themselves. As a matter of fact, if we would re-read the chapter, we would notice that the critics really have not attacked Jesus directly at all! But the point of the whole incident is the evangelist's way of showing what a sign is in the Johannine sense: a work that Jesus performs to show his divinity to the eyes of faith. The subtle interplay of Johannine irony and the incredible resistance of "the Jews" makes little sense in the light of the simple truth! This is the evangelist's way of fleshing out what he summarized in the Prologue: ". . . his own did not accept him" (Jn 1:11).

B. The New Manna (ch. 6)

The sign of the loaves is one of the few elements of the Public Ministry tradition that the fourth evangelist shares with all three Synoptics. It is not difficult to see why; the Church had developed its practice of sharing the eucharistic memorial in such a way, that this ritual had become an indispensable part of the collective life style of the Christian people. From this perspective it was only natural for the evangelists to trace in their Gospels the scene which anticipates the eucharist, as Jesus gives an advance sign of his intention to feed his people with new manna. As a matter of fact, Mark and Matthew both describe the miracle of the loaves twice, but this seems to be because they both preserve doublets, or variant forms of the tradition, so that at first glance it appears as if Jesus performed this sign twice.

Gradually, as we read the whole chapter, we see how the fourth evangelist has framed the incident in his own distinctive way. As he did with the healing sign in chapter 5, likewise here he follows up the sign with a lengthy discourse in which Jesus interprets his own action. But there is another clue, which comes right at the beginning of the chapter, in the reference to the Passover feast, in 6:4. None of the Synoptics associates the loaves' miracle with the Passover. So this clue helps us to follow the Johannine mind and its special pattern. The passover was the annual celebration of the Exodus, in which God liberated his people from Egyptian slavery and sustained them in the desert by providing manna for their food. The fourth evangelist shows Jesus offering to the crowd the sign of the loaves as a lesson to teach them that he is the new manna, just as he has already presented himself as the new Temple (2:12-25) and as the giver of new life (3:1-12). And in the Bread of Life Discourse which follows the sign, Jesus speaks also of the necessity of eating his flesh and drinking his blood, but the Fourth Gospel has no narrative of Jesus instituting the sacrament of the eucharistic memorial at the Last Supper, as the Synoptics have! The fourth evangelist has concentrated all of his eucharistic theology in this one chapter. And as we read the chapter, we can see that he has done it well.

The Signs (6:1-21)

As the narrative opens against the backdrop of the coming Passover festival, nobody except Jesus appears to know what is happening (6:6). The disciples are not expecting anything special. The crowds respond to the sign in the wrong way: after eating the miraculous food, they enthusiastically acclaim Jesus as the new Moses, and they prepare to recognize him as a new messianic king. This is flattering enough, but it is not at all what Jesus wants. He moves away from them. Any appearance of temporal or political ambition would blur his image and cause people to miss the lesson that he wants them to learn.

The sign of the water-walk is also in the Synoptic Gospels, in association with the loaves miracle. But it is a private sign, for the disciples only, not for general consumption by the crowds. The subtle Johannine mind works here too, showing the gentle way in which Jesus reassures the frightened disciples, as he joins them and brings their difficult ride to a successful conclusion. John probably speaks again here from his own reminiscences of what he had personally experienced long before. He has perhaps asked himself many times, why had they been afraid (6:19, 20)? They still had much to learn!

The Crowd (6:22-24)

It is difficult to reconstruct the narrative scene here, because the evangelist is concentrating so intensely on the theological points that he wants to make, that he is less successful with the details of the scene. Nevertheless, we can see the crowd, who are so impressed and thrilled by the sign of the loaves that they pursue Jesus as far as Capernaum, hoping to have more of the same. This is another indication of the fact that only Jesus really understands what has been signified by the Passover loaves.

The Bread of Life Discourse (6:25-58)

6:25-34   The scene has shifted to the synagogue in Capernaum (6:59), as Jesus again takes the initiative, this time to challenge and correct the limited vision of the faceless crowd. The whole dialogue is a working-through of the ironic obtuseness of the crowd, who never succeed in breaking through their own sense-bound level of understanding to arrive at the spiritual reality of Jesus' lesson.

Immediately Jesus goes to the core of their misunderstanding: you should be looking for spiritual food—the kind that nourishes you to eternal life! You are short-sighted when you want merely to see a repeat of the loaves sign! They question him again, and he challenges them to make the effort of faith, which will bring them beyond the level of their senses. This shifts the entire level of the dialogue to the level that Jesus wants to maintain. He associates his sign of the loaves with Moses and his manna-sign. But both of these signs are only that—signs, not the reality itself! The real food that they need is not either of these, but these signs should prepare them for the real-life-giving food, which is sent to them from heaven by the provident Father.

6:35-50   The second part of the dialogue revolves around the mysterious identity of Jesus himself as the new manna, which surpasses both Moses' manna and even the sign of the barley loaves. Still, as usual, the crowds fail to grasp the invisible essence of the message, because they see only the human dimension of Jesus, "the son of Joseph" (6:42). The pedagogy of faith should lead these people by progressive stages, from the desert manna, to the sign of the loaves, and then to the person of Jesus himself. And here again Jesus speaks of himself in both the heaven-to-earth pattern and in that of earth-to heaven, as he did in his conversation with Nicodemus (ch. 3). He is the teacher and the life-giver, who descends from heaven to offer the gift of his teaching, along with the challenging demand that men should accept it by responding to him on the level of faith. Such a response would make them share now in the eternal life which Jesus shares with the Father, and orients them toward the consummation which they will achieve "on the last day" (6:39-40); then they will pass through death, beyond earth and time, to the fullness of their final destiny. This will be the earth-to-heaven direction which will complete the gift of eternal life by bringing believers to the presence of both the life-giving Father, and the raised-up Son.

John's eucharistic doctrine is not connected here with the Last Supper, or with any mention of Calvary. But Jesus' word about his plan to raise up believers on the last day, is his promise that this "communion" with him will lead believers to share his resurrection glory. Indeed, the "raising up" that Jesus offers to believers (6:39-40) is the same as what the Father has prepared for him! So there can be no true fellowship with Jesus which will not lead to resurrection, because the only Jesus who exists is the raised-up Lord—the Lamb of God (1:29).

6:51-59   At the well in Samaria Jesus offered living water; now he offers living bread. Both of these, obviously, are metaphors, or parables. But now Jesus moves from parable to sacrament, as he takes the crowd deeper into the mystery of his plan. He draws not only from the background of the manna sign, but also from the biblical images of the messianic banquet, which he suggested already at Cana (Is 25:6-7; 55:1-3), and of wisdom's banquet (Pr 9:1-6; Si 24:17-21), both of which speak of God's gifts under the image of food and drink. All of this background has served John well, as he has studied his experience of Jesus in the light of the Scriptures and of the life style of the primitive Church and its eucharistic experience. John's special view of the flesh and blood of Jesus speaks of having eternal life now, and having even more of it later. The church's sacramental pattern has translated this into the eucharistic meal, which unifies all these biblical themes in the concrete reality of its ritual, and in which it celebrates the prospect of its own promised consummation.

The Response (6:60-71)

The manna was from the past; the messianic banquet was an image of the future; wisdom's banquet was for the limited few. It is no wonder that they were unprepared for such a suggestion! Was it a call to human cannibalism, or a promulgation of divine wisdom? One was too far beneath them, and the other was too far above them! So they did the human thing; they protested and walked away (6:60, 66). And why not? The pattern has become clear enough by now; the unspeakable gift is available free of charge, for those who allow themselves to be led by the leader (6:45). But they do not; instead, they stumble (6:61) and fall back to the comfortable blindness of their domesticated and earth-bound religion. A sad response indeed.

Still, the crisis brings out the best in the twelve, who appear to be learning, if with difficulty. Peter speaks for all of them, and makes his confession of faith—not at Caesarea Philippi, as Mark and Matthew have it, but here, as a counterbalance to the unconverted loaf-seekers of Capernaum! The Christians of John's Ephesian church must have gotten the point of Jesus' searing and demanding question (6:67). This is our chance. Drop it now, or else join Peter and go all the way.

Yet, even here, Jesus is on top of the situation, as he was at the beginning of the chapter (6:6) as well as at the beginning of his Public Ministry (2:24-25). Now (6:64-65; 70-71) he is not flattered by human nature, and he never begs for acceptance. The unfaith which persecuted him and plotted for his life at the pool (5:16-18) begins to mature into the concreteness of treachery, which Judas represents and which, for all its secrecy, is no surprise to the Lord (6:70-71).

Questions for Consideration and Reflection

1. How do these chapters advance the theology of the Gospel beyond the content of chs. 1-4?
2. Is the evangelist effective in showing the connection between the feasts and the signs?
3. What does the evangelist mean by "life?"
4. How do the discourse sections in these chapters relate to the signs which precede them?
5. What special lessons is the evangelist trying to present to his contemporaries in these chapters?
6. How do the "signs" of this Gospel compare to the miracles of the Synoptics?

7

THE UNWELCOME LIGHT

"So he said to them, 'When you lift up the Son of Man, you will know that 'I am who I am;' then you will know that I do nothing on my own authority, but I say only what the Father has instructed me to say' "
                                                          (Jn 8:28).

Preliminary Reading

Read Jn chs. 7-10. This section is somewhat longer and more subtle than the previous ones have been. Be prepared to re-read it several times, jotting down your remarks as things come to your attention. Notice especially these details:

7:2; 10:22 the feasts;
7:11-13; 10:19-21, 31-33 the various reactions to Jesus;
7:31-59; 8:28 Jesus' relationship to Abraham;
7:33-34; 10:14-18 Jesus' hints about the future;
Ch. 9 The dualism involved in the cure of the blind man;
7:37-38; 8:12; 9:5; 10:1-18 Jesus' parables.

As he moves further into the fabric of his message, the fourth evangelist undertakes to prepare his friends more and more specifically for the coming scenes of Jesus' death, and for the lessons of its significance. The atmosphere of approaching death becomes noticeable now, while the mood of tension and confrontation becomes sustained and constant. Nevertheless, in the face of it, Jesus is always supremely self-possessed, never threatened or defensive, and in control of both himself and the basic situation. All of this comes through between the lines, and it is very much part of the substance of the evangelist's message, which he directs to his Ephesian friends, no less than the narrative itself is.

A. The Booths Feast (7:1-13)

The feast of Booths (or Tabenacles) was one of the three pilgrimage festivals, which pious Jews were expected to celebrate in Jerusalem. During the ancient time of Moses and the desert wandering, the Hebrew ancestors had maintained a nomadic life style of living in tents. After they became settled in the Land of Canaan, they developed agriculture, and with that came harvest festivals. In the course of time the harvest celebration became associated with the primordial memory of the Exodus wandering. This led to a combining of the two elements, as later generations of Jews constructed booths, or huts (tabernacles), in which they lived for the week-long duration of the festival, observing the prescriptions of Lv 23 and Dt 16. By Jesus' time it had become customary to celebrate the festival by making the pilgrimage to the capital and joining in the liturgical ceremonies there, which included both water rites and illuminations of the Temple area by huge flaming torches. In these chapters of the Fourth Gospel we see several subtle clues which allude to the various aspects of this annual festival.

We can imagine the crowded situation in Jerusalem during this festival week. This, of course, prepares us for the crowds who will be there at the time of the final Passover, and call for Jesus' blood; also for the crowds of "Cretans and Arabs" and "devout Jews of every nation under heaven" who will be there for the first Christian Pentecost (Ac 2:5, 11).

There seems to be some uncertainty about whether Jesus should attend the festival in Jerusalem. He is having trouble enough in Galilee, since even his own family have little understanding of who he is, or what he is doing. Furthermore, the crowds who saw and ate the new manna at the multiplication of the loaves, have not understood the sign or responded with faith. Beyond this, Jesus' first visit to the capital brought him persecution and a desire for his death on the part of "the Jews" (5:16-18).

We get the impression that Jesus' relatives saw him as a potential leader of some kind of political rebellion; this is why they suggest that he should go down to Judea and show himself and his power there. But again the fourth evangelist shows the contrast of two mindsets that never meet. Jesus knows that this is not his purpose, and that this kind of motive should not govern him or his movements. He goes eventually, but not for the reason that they mistakenly propose to him. Jesus knows too that it is not yet time for his definitive visit to the holy city, during which he will be "glorified" and "lifted up." That, when it comes, will be "the hour." But, for this, "It is not yet the right time" (7:6).

The crowds are neutral but curious, while "the Jews" (as the fourth evangelist calls the unbelieving leaders) are hostile and succeed in dividing and intimidating their own countrymen.

A Case of Mistaken Identity (7:14-36)

We see here an intertwining of the incredulity of the leaders, and the lack of understanding on the part of the crowds. The one group are implacably hostile, while the others are more neutral. Jesus faces them both with a message about his own identity. This is always the message of the Beloved Disciple, whether it comes in Jesus' own words and works, or through the interpretation of the Apostle, as it did in the First Johannine Epistle.

After the festival has been underway for a few days, Jesus presents himself teaching in the Temple, which he challenged and cleansed during his previous visit, (2:12-25). What does he teach? The evangelist does not say explicitly, but it must have been enough to impress Jesus' hearers. He was not a professional rabbi, but he speaks like a well-educated intellectual—a man of letters.

But again they misunderstand. Jesus is more than a rabbi, because his teaching is above that of Moses and the Law. What Jesus teaches is directly from the Father—after all, is he not the Word made flesh, the only-begotten One, ever at the Father's side (1:14, 18)?

The great tragedy is that these people have such a rigid and narrow idea of religion that they are unable to allow that God should operate outside the limits of their own expectations. Of course Moses spoke of the Sabbath rest (Ex 20:8-11; Dt 5:12-15); but Jesus is not limited by this, or prevented by it from healing a crippled man on the holy day (ch. 5). They would circumcise a newborn child on the Sabbath; can the one sent from God not give life and healing on a day of man's rest? A little common sense should be allowed to prevail here.

7:25-36   From this the scene shifts to a play on the themes of *from where* Jesus has come, and *to where* he is about to go. In each instance the same abyss reappears, as Jesus speaks on a heavenly and spiritual plane, while his interlocutors, both "the crowds" and "the Jews" understand—or misunderstand—on the merely earthly level of their sense-experience. This is what makes them fail to see that Jesus' origin is not a matter of a town or a family tree, but of the eternal self of the Father, from whose presence he has come to them. Likewise they fail to grasp Jesus' suggestion—which Jesus makes now for the first time in the Fourth Gospel (7:33)—that he is to go away—to the same Father who is his origin. But instead of rising to the lofty level of his words, they think horizontally of geography, and miss the point (7:35-36). But the evangelist's subtle suggestion is a compliment to his Ephesian Christian friends, who are Greeks, gentiles of the world outside Israel, and whose faith-response to Jesus he hopes to strengthen and sustain by this message.

Come to the Water! (7:37-52)

Water and Spirit give life. This was Jesus' message to Nicodemus (3:3-5); it will also be part of the message of Calvary (Jn 19:30-34). Jesus' use of this terminology at the end of the week of Booths (7:37-38) may have been his way of challenging the sufficiency of the water-rite, which the priests performed in Jerusalem, carrying vessels of water from the Siloam pool to the Temple altar in solemn procession.

Jesus must have made a scene powerful enough to get people's attention, and to remain in the memory of the Beloved Disciple, whose description of the incident we have here. Yet, apparently, they did not understand. However, in the light of the pierced side of Jesus at Calvary, and of the Holy Spirit given at Pentecost as well as of the baptismal liturgy which had evolved in succeeding decades, John had gradually come to see how Jesus' words on that closing day of the festival week had been a promise of living realities. The real life of men comes from Jesus to baptized Christians, not from the pool of Siloam—or from the feast of Booths at all.

Now the drama intensifies. The bitterness which responded to Jesus on his first visit to Jerusalem (5:16-18), matures now into a plot to arrest him (7:30). But, as the chapter opened (7:6-8), so it closes (7:45-46): the time is not ripe—"the hour" has not yet arrived. Jesus will be taken and "lifted up" when he is ready, and not before. Yet, even here, the evangelist is effective in depicting the contrast between the unyielding intolerance of the leaders, especially of the chief priests and of the pharisaical teachers. He does well also in depicting the temple guards, who respect Jesus (7:46), even though they do not arrive at conversion.

New Light Unseen (8:12-30)

Another part of the liturgy of Booths was the lighting of the entire area of the Temple with four huge lampstands of torches. Under these lampstands the priests and levites led a solemn ritual of dancing and singing the Psalms of Ascent (Ps 124-130), as we learn from the rabbinical texts of the *Mishnah*.

All very impressive. But this kind of light is dim—even dark—in comparison to the brightness which Jesus has to offer—the light of life (8:12). Again, his message is the same as it always is in the Johannine message—a call to have faith in Jesus' own person as the dispenser of the Father's gift of life. And again the familiar Johannine device of dualism appears in the contrast of opposites: this time the light challenges the darkness, just as flesh challenged spirit in 3:6, and heaven challenged earth in 3:12.

But, in doing this, Jesus witnesses to himself, and, again, the leaders respond, not by faith, but by invoking an irrelevant section of the Mosaic tradition. The rules about witnessing to truth are in Dt 17:6; 19:15, and in Nb 35:30. They all require the testimony of at least two witnesses for establishing a truth of fact. But, just as they have done consistently, these benighted leaders of the blind do not see the spiritual truth that now challenges them, since Jesus and the Father are the two witnesses that offer the light of truth. But they can see no truth because they can see no light. This is the failure of the Pharisees, who were so devoted to the letter of the Law, that they lost sight of the light of life because it was bigger than their preconceived idea of religion.

8:21-30   More and more the evangelist works toward what is to come, as he presents Jesus speaking again of his imminent departure (8:21), as he did shortly before (7:33-34). We recall that he also told the disciples at the Last Supper that he was to leave them (Jn 14:2-4; 16:5-16). But we can see a great difference between the two tellings. Jesus tells the disciples, "It is much better for you that I go . . . the Paraclete will come to you . . . I will send him to you" (16:7). John has seen the whole thing from long after the fact. The departure of Jesus led to the coming of the Holy Spirit to the Church—to those who relate to Jesus by faith, even though he is absent now. But his departure has left the unbelieving leaders even worse off than they were before he challenged them to believe in him. Now, as before, they are without the gift of sonship and life, which they have rejected. But, even beyond that, they are now in the darkness of having no prospect of future glory, no assurance of heaven. The only way for them to escape from the enclosing hopelessness of sin and death, is to accept the message that Jesus has been presenting, i.e. that, as he tells them in 8:24, "I AM!"

We have here Jesus' first use of this puzzling formula, but he will repeat it in 8:28 and in 8:58, as well as again in 13:19. The phrase seems simple enough by itself. But when we recognize that it is a Greek equivalent of the Hebrew words which God spoke to Moses in the burning bush incident (Ex 3:14), then we see that the evangelist presents Jesus here challenging the leaders to accept him as Jahweh God, present and speaking to them.

No wonder that this was more than they could absorb! It had never happened to them before! They saw no precedent; no man ever claimed what God had claimed. The one who faces them and says now, "I AM!" is the same one who spoke to Moses in the bush. We wonder how we would have reacted if we had been there.

Yet, it will all take its course. Jesus will be "lifted up" (8:28), both in the apparent shame of crucifixion, and in the divine reality of resurrection glory. When this happens, the full reality will be that the Father is the one who is working in their very presence, although they have not been able to pass beyond the veil of their senses to see it with the eyes of faith. Jesus repeats here a formula which he used in his fruitless dialogue with Nicodemus (3:14-15), and he will use it again as almost the last word of his Public Ministry (12:32). The phrase captivates our attention here because of its very ambiguity. Jesus, "lifted up" in crucifixion, will appear to be the supreme failure. Yet, the whole thrust of the Johannine message to the Ephesian church is that this "lifted up" Lord is king, glorified in resurrection and in his return to the Father, as he now calls for their loyalty in faith. The evangelist's closing words in 8:30 appear to be directed primarily at these Ephesian friends, to give them a not-too-subtle hint, that they too should see the futility of such unbelief, and do better.

Who is Father? (8:31-59)

As the confrontation continues, we see a play on the theme of "Who is father?" After Jesus has promised freedom as the fruit of truth, his hostile interlocutors reject his offer on the ground that they are already free, because of their pride in being Jews and Abraham's children. Indeed, their claim has some merit, since this very consciousness of their history and of their collective identity had sustained these people through the trials and pressures of almost two millenia. Yet, by the same token, the Johannine irony shows up once again, linked here with the related use of dualism, to contrast the earthly father with the heavenly one, and the limited vision of the one level, with the fuller view of the other. Those who do not possess the real freedom of real truth, are not sons of God, or of Abraham but slaves of sin, the deadening power of evil that binds men to the short-range things of earth and sense-life, and prevents them from relating successfully—filially—as sons to God as Father.

They resent the searing penetration of Jesus' words, however, precisely because he strikes at the self-deception that they consider to be their strong point. If they are so sure that they are in the right and that he is in the wrong, why are they so anxious to destroy him? Let the truth show itself! But the fact that they cannot bear to endure him, shows that they are unwilling to admit their need of what he offers. This resistance to the truth shows that they are ruled by falsehood, and thus by Satan, who is the father of lies (8:44).

So, there are three fathers involved, God, Abraham and Satan. One is heavenly, the giver of life, truth and freedom. One is earthly, the giver of natural life to his descendants who are the chosen people. The third is the prince of darkness and the father of all that is false and evil. There is really no opposition between the fatherhood of God and that of Abraham; they are merely on different levels. But because these leaders oppose one to the other instead of accepting both, they miss the truth and show themselves to be bound by the diabolical power of evil which really governs their lives.

They become defensive again, and throw back to Jesus the suggestions that he, rather than themselves, is the one possessed and governed by evil power (7:20; 8:48, 53; 9:20; 10:20). Even here, however, the truth defeats them. Jesus, who has claimed to be greater than Moses, the Temple and the manna, now claims to be greater than Abraham! Here too the irony appears, as "the Jews" see no further than the venerable antiquity of Abraham, whose prestige is the greater for his being the first of the Patriarchs and the uniquely privileged ancestor. Even beyond this greatness of the ancient ancestor is the timeless eternity of the one who said "I AM!" Again, as earlier, in this same chapter, Jesus says what only God has ever said. We probably do not reflect enough on the stunning novelty of this situation. No prophet or other man, however worthy, has ever said such a thing. So it should not surprise us that Jesus' claim surprises them! And they understood his claim for what it was, for otherwise they would not have resisted so strongly, or else Jesus would have modified his position. But he means what he says, and they know what he means! But it is too much to accept. Such a claim strikes them as blasphemy, and calls for stoning (8:59; 10:30-33). The other possibility, of course, is that what Jesus says is true. And this is the alternative that the evangelist offers to his friends, as he works to make them see what Israel's leaders could not see.

Who is Blind? (9:1-41)

The theme of *light* continues in the narrative of the sixth sign, as Jesus heals the man who has been blind all his life. We suspect that the evangelist is influenced in the telling, by the painful experience of Jewish Christians, who have found themselves persecuted and ostracized by their countrymen (as Paul was), because of their new faith in Jesus. These factors, along with the familiar Johannine patterns which we find here as well as elsewhere in the fabric of the Fourth Gospel, show how this miracle story has been amplified well beyond the more restrained miracle stories of the Synoptic writers. Mark, Matthew and Luke show Jesus' miracles as works of messianic healing, which announce the arrival of God's promised reign, and call for conversion and a reformed life style. John's Gospel presents fewer miracle stories than any of the Synoptics, and presents them as signs which should bolster the faith of its Christian receivers, and encourage them to persevere in the face of error within the Church, and of persecution from without it.

One of Jesus' most trenchant, if not cryptic, sayings, occurs in 9:3-5, and these words explain Jesus' reason for taking the initiative, unsolicited, and working this sign. The man's blindness is not a punishment for anything; it is, rather, the raw material that God will use to show his own light-and-life-giving goodness. Jesus will use this sign as a symbol of himself, which people will be able to recall later, when it will seem, to merely human eyes, that the darkness has overcome the light. Then they can remember the ease and self-possession with which Jesus healed the man, to show that he alone is the source of the world's real light (9:5), which is the power to see the spiritual reality of God. Thus the power of seeing which the man gains, is also a symbol of the light of faith, which he eventually shows by his act of homage to Jesus (9:38).

The ones who come off looking poorest in this drawn-out but excellently sustained drama, are the man's parents, and, of course, "the pharisees" and "the Jews." Perhaps it would not be quite so bad if they had some good reason for their failure, but they appear unmasked in their sheer moral weakness. These parents are the victims of human respect, as the evangelist explains in his parenthesis (9:22-23), and they lack the backbone which would make them answer with some conviction. Instead, they forfeit their opportunity to make a profession of faith in Jesus, and they pass the challenge to their son. Here the evangelist seems to be using the figure of the parents as a counterfoil, in order to show to his Christian friends a negative example of how they should *not* act under the pressure of persecution. He will allude again to this pattern in 12:42, where he ranks these fearful parents along with such leaders as Nicodemus, who also fell short of faith, and came to Jesus by night because of his fear of being seen (3:2; also 7:50-52). The leaders and "the Jews" also look poor here, but perhaps not more so than they have looked, especially in the previous scenes of chs. 7-8. They represent the really blind.

The really fortunate and successful one is the man whom Jesus healed, because he not only received the gift of sight, but he sees his cure as a divine sign, and responds in faith. He has come to have the best of both worlds! As Jesus says, "God's works show forth in him" (9:3). No less truly, John prepares his followers for the coming night (9:4), which will be the time of Jesus' death (13:30).

Sheepgate and Shepherd (10:1-21)

When we come to these words of Jesus about himself, we wonder how they relate to the whole scene which the evangelist has been presenting. The "sheepgate" and "shepherd" passage seems curiously out of place here, so that we may conjecture that it represents either a momentary shift of thought—a sort of aside or parenthesis—on the part of the evangelist, or perhaps an insertion placed here by a later editor. In any case it is probably one of the most familiar passages of any of the Gospels, even though many Christians who have drawn consolation from it may not know that it is part of the Fourth Gospel.

The shepherd image, of course, is not new with these words of Jesus. It occurs frequently in the Old Testament, not only in the familiar Psalm 23, but also in the prophetic oracles of Isaiah (40:11); Jeremiah (23:1 ff.; 31:10); Ezekiel (34:12-23; 37:24) and Zechariah (11:4-17; 13:7). In these OT passages the image means various things, and refers to various persons, sometimes to God, sometimes to good or bad leaders of Israel. But when Jesus applies the figure to himself, he sets himself here over against the pharisees and other leaders of Israel, who fail to provide adequately—and with self-giving generosity—for the spiritual life of their countrymen.

This metaphor, or parable, has a number of meanings. Jesus describes himself first of all (10:1-5) as the genuine shepherd, who knows the sheep and is recognized by them so that he is not a fake or a robber, who sneaks up on them by deceit. The real key to this part of the parable is in v. 5: Jesus speaks of the trust and confidence which binds the sheep to the genuine shepherd, because they know that only he really cares for their welfare.

In the next few verses (10:7-10) Jesus shifts the metaphor somewhat, and speaks of himself as the gate. If the sheep enter through the right gate, they will be safe within the fold, or enclosure, and when they exit by this way, they will find good pasture. Other gates lead to other places, but not to the right ones. The contrast becomes all the more vivid when we see Jesus here comparing himself again to the entrenched but inadequate leaders, who claim to preach true religion in Israel, but fail to bring their people to the living reality of God!

This much we can well imagine Jesus saying at the Booths festival, to challenge everyone who might hear him. It is difficult to imagine that they would not get the point, even though they might not like it. But surely the leaders would recognize Jesus' challenge to their religious authenticity, and to their authority. As for the crowds in general, it seems, as the evangelist says in 10:19-21, that at least some of them got the message: What Jesus does is good and life-giving; how can what he says be bad?

Even beyond this, the evangelist gives more words of Jesus which hint toward the future (10:14-18)—even though John, teaching with the advantage of hindsight, has learned to recognize the connection between Jesus' words and the later events which may not have been apparent to him when he first heard the words. When Jesus speaks of himself as the shepherd who is so solicitous for the sheep that he will die willingly to protect them from death, he prepares his hearers again, more explicitly than before, for what is soon to come. Then his further reference to "other sheep that do not belong to this fold" (v. 16) but which will belong to "one flock then, one shepherd," is another encouraging compliment to John's gentile converts who hear this from the Apostle's teaching in Ephesus. They did not belong to the original fold of Israel, but now they are all members of one flock, which makes no distinction between Jews and gentiles. Here again, the bigness of Jesus' view contrasts with the smallness and nationalist exclusivism of these leaders, who limit God to Israel—their way.

We may usually think of Jesus' parables as stories which he tells in the Synoptic Gospels to describe the Kingdom of God. But here we find a larger meaning of Jesus' parables, as he speaks of himself in the Fourth Gospel as *bread, light, shepherd, gate*, and later on as *the way, truth and life* (14:6), and then of *the vine and the branches* (ch. 15). So a parable is not always a story. It is a word-picture, typical of the Semitic and Oriental style of speaking, which uses images from everyday life and draws lessons from them. Some parables are stories, some are only phrases. But Jesus uses them all so effectively, that after twenty centuries he still relates to our imagination, as the master-preacher, starting out from the simple things of our ordinary experience, and using them to teach us the lofty things of the Father, of eternity, and of divine life, which he came to offer us.

B. *The Dedication (10:22-39)*

Another feast brings Jesus to the capital again, on another pilgrimage. The Dedication, or *Hanukkah* feast, commemorates the Maccabees, who re-captured and re-dedicated the Temple and the altar which had been ritually defiled by the Greeks about two hundred years before Jesus (1 M:1-4). The evangelist describes this visit of Jesus and the tensions which it occasions, more briefly than the preceding one, which is the longest of all his cameos of feasts and signs. Lights and torches were a major part of this celebration, which still occurs nowadays, as it did then, in December—the winter, as the evangelist says in passing (10:22).

There are no neutral crowds this time, and there is no sign. The entire scene is another confrontation between Jesus and "the Jews." He, not they, can give true life—eternal life—to Israel. Only he can give them God's deathless life, because he and the Father are one (10:30).

Another devastating claim! It must be either blasphemous, or true! The greatest person in Israel's sacred history was Moses, and he was never more than prophet and servant of God. Now this obscure Nazarene, with his claims, puts Moses in the shade. It is not so surprising that they reach for the rocks, even though Jesus can show that his words are fully in accord with the Scriptures (Ps 82:6). He knows the Scriptures better than they do, because he knows them as God's gift of spirit and life, whereas these leaders have reduced them to a dead letter, which they have unwittingly made into an end in itself.

The evangelist draws this brief encounter scene to a close with a reprise, which summarizes Jesus' challenge to all. Believe my works, which show the Father in me (10:37-38). A cloud of tragedy concludes the incident, as these leaders, defeated by their own blindness, renew their attempt to destroy the One who is one with the Father. But they cannot. The "hour" has not yet come.

Questions for Consideration and Reflection

1. How does the fourth evangelist show the relationship between Jesus and the feasts of Booths and of the Dedication?
2. What examples of irony and of dualism are evident in these chapters?
3. Why does the evangelist repeatedly emphasize the unbelief of Jesus' countrymen?
4. How does the evangelist present Jesus' parables?
5. How does the healing of the blind man relate to the Booths festival?
6. What is a sign, in the Johannine sense?
7. How does Jesus allude to the future in these chapters?

8

TOWARDS THE
GREAT PASSOVER

"For your sakes I am glad I was not there,
that you may come to believe" (Jn 11:15).

Preliminary Reading

Read Jn 11-12, with an eye to the transition from Jesus' Public Ministry to the Great Passover of his Glorification. Write down your observations, and also any questions which may come to your mind as you read. Notice especially the following details:

11:4,15,42 Jesus' reason for raising Lazarus;
11:22-24,33 The limited expectations of Martha and Mary;
11:45-54   The reaction of the leaders to the sign;
12:7-8   The intensifying atmosphere of Jesus' coming death and departure;
12:23-36   The special themes in the dialogue/monologue;
12:37-43   The evangelist's summary and evaluation of Jesus' ministry of signs.

Lazarus (11:1-44)

The fourth evangelist is the only one who speaks of Jesus' act of bringing the dead Lazarus back to life. We have the parable in Luke's Gospel (ch. 16) about Lazarus and the rich man, but there is no similarity between the two men aside from that of their names. Furthermore, there are so many clues in this section, that we need not doubt that the evangelist intends to present this seventh sign—the greatest and last of the series—as Jesus' way of preparing people for his own death, and for his conquest of it in his resurrection. The atmosphere of death which began to build up in the Booths section (7:1, 19-20, 30-36; 10:15-18) becomes much more noticeable now, but it is always conquered death, which holds no power and brings no fear.

Martha and Mary apparently expect Jesus to hurry to Bethany and heal his sick friend immediately after receiving their message. But they show no indication at all that they know what Jesus is planning to do. He is in control of the situation again, and he seems to delay deliberately (11:6), instead of rushing to Judea. His curing of the sick has already been spectacular enough (chs. 5, 9); but to bring a man from the tomb four days after his death—who would expect him to do that? The dead Lazarus, like the blind man at the Booths feast, will serve God by being a public example of Jesus' life-giving and healing power—another sign! No need to avoid Judea and its hostile leaders; the "hour" of night-darkness is approaching, true enough—but it has not yet come (11:9-10), and the light is still on earth (9:4-5).

There is something almost humorous about Jesus' calm purposefulness here, in the face of the more modest expectations of the two sisters, and the fearfulness and pessimism of even his own disciples (11:8, 16). Both sisters come out and rebuke Jesus for delaying (11:21, 32). Martha shares the pious confidence of her countrymen, who in recent centuries have begun to look ahead to resurrection and judgment of the dead (Ps 16:10; 73:23; Dn 12:1-3; 2M 6-7; 12:14), even though the Sadducees ridicule this insight into God's plan and his justice (Mk 12:18-27). But there is no need for Martha to wait until the last day, for the end of the world. The light is here now, in front of her. Jesus goes beyond her expectations and claims what can be a prerogative only of God (11:25). No need for Jesus to ask God for anything—only for Martha to give to Jesus the faith-response that he demands. Resurrection and life can come only from the One who is Lord of life and death, and this is what Jesus is now claiming for himself. Did Martha understand what Jesus was claiming to be, or what he was planning to do, or why he was planning to do it, or what he wanted them to learn from it all—or what we should learn from it? Somehow, even her profession of faith seems too hesitant (11:27). The Messiah and Son of God coming into the world could be a king, a political leader sent by God to restore Israel's lost temporal glory. Others had seen this much in Jesus' signs (6:15; 7:4). But what he plans to give now is more and bigger than that! But they have to be big enough and bold enough to let God work, and make their brother for all time to come a living symbol of what all men can draw from Jesus—resurrection and life—*now*.

We may wonder why Jesus should be troubled (11:33-35). Was this a rare display of his humanity—his tender regard for his deceased friend, or his sympathy for this family who have befriended him and now suffer in bereavement? Or was it a protest at their limitations, and their too modest expectations? Even the bystanders reproach, but expect too little, because they believe too little (11:37). Yet, while the humanity of the situation troubles him, he turns from it to commune with the Father in a brief prayer (11:41-42), in which he repeats his own intention (11:4) that all this is to show a glowing sign of God's presence, enough to call forth faith in all that Jesus has claimed to be. How odd that all this should be "for the sake of the crowd" (11:42), and not only for the bereaved sisters—but if it had been only for them, we would not know the challenge that it presents to us! This is another indication of the evangelist's intention, to present this sign as a proximate introduction to Jesus' great conquest of death which will soon begin to unfold.

Reactions (11:45-52)

The evangelist describes the reaction of the leaders so graphically, that he seems to have overheard their discussion. The other explanation, and the more likely one, is that, as he has done before (2:18-22; 7:39), he combines the narrative of the event with an interpretation of it which he has come to understand only many years later. These chief priests and pharisees are again a counterfoil, because they react in exactly the way in which the evangelist wants his Christian friends *not* to react. Instead of responding to Jesus with the faith which this sign was intended to evoke (11:47), these leaders show two things: first, their own persistent unfaith, and, secondly, the ironic way in which unknowingly and without realizing it, Caiaphas and the others whom he led as High Priest, acted like a prophet, interpreting his own failure as a part of the Father's plan! After the Roman counter-attack had levelled Jerusalem in 70 A.D., Christians read this later event in the light of Israel's earlier rejection of Jesus (Lk 21:20-22). But by this time the Church had also become more gentile than Jewish, so that Israel's negative attitude to the gift which Jesus had offered, eventually came to appear as a necessary part of the great mystery of salvation which came to "all the dispersed children of God" (11:52). Caiaphas did realize what he was saying, but, from his mature perspective, long after the fact, our evangelist shows God writing straight with the crooked lines of human failure.

The Great Passover Approaches (11:53-57)

The die is cast now, and we see a curious interplay of the themes of *life* and *death*. Jesus has brought life to the dead Lazarus, and this act is the "last straw," which will bring on his own death at the hands of those who have failed to believe in him and are therefore dead in their sins (8:24). But this act of death will bring life to others, whose faith attaches them to the person of Jesus, and to the power of his resurrection.

As the Passover time comes on, and the crowds approach Jerusalem for the sacrifices and celebrations of their collective birth in the ancient Exodus, the supreme confrontation is about to occur. Jesus is a wanted man, but an unwanted God.

The Woman with the Nard (12:1-11)

Now that the crucial Passover season has arrived, the Fourth Gospel comes closer to the Synoptic Gospels, all three of which also tell of the woman and her oil (Mk 14; Mt 26). Luke, however, places the scene earlier in Jesus' Public Ministry (Lk 7), with no overtone of Passover, or of death and burial. The Johannine picture of the incident is as complimentary to the woman as it is critical of Judas, whom the evangelist presents here for the first time (although Jesus has alluded to him briefly in 6:70-71), as the moral failure which he has always epitomized throughout Christian history. And poor Lazarus—he is now a wanted man too (12:10). What an unenviable position—to be caught in the tension between God and men. What a strange coincidence it all is now—so long after, and so far away. Lazarus, who says not a word, is remembered and envied, while the sophisticated leaders, and poor Judas—and Pontius Pilate too, for that matter—go down in history as unrehabilitated failures who unknowingly helped God to do what they did not expect him to do, and missed their chance to share in his gift.

Palm Sunday (12:12-19)

Again the Johannine Gospel comes closer to the Synoptics, since all four evangelists describe Jesus' triumphant—if misunderstood— entry into the capital. But again the Johannine memory is independent in recalling and describing the scene. Mark and Matthew place the anointing at Bethany after Palm Sunday, and they both speak of Jesus' cursing of the fig tree. All three Synoptics describe Jesus' cleansing of the Temple in connection with the messianic entry on Palm Sunday. But our evangelist concentrates here on the single scene of the entry itself, although he associates it with the crowd who witnessed to the raising of Lazarus (12:17).

The whole scene shows Jesus towering above and beyond everyone else, although the significance of the incident must have come home to John only much later (12:16). All of the power of the incident is contained in the two quotations from the Scripture. The first one (12:13) repeats a royal victory greeting from Ps 118:25-26, and implies all the enthusiasm which originally went with the celebration of the Israelite king's triumph in battle. In the light of the signs which Jesus has worked, and of the claims and demands which he has made, this kind of acclamation seems only fitting. But the fact that Jesus used a humble donkey, and then took on such unimaginable abuse from the same crowd only a few days later, could only add up to the mysterious picture of the humble king of Zechariah's oracle (Zc 9:9). Yet, the mind of Jesus and that of the crowd never meet! His signs, and the most recent ones most especially, enthuse them to expect a renewal of the temporal autonomy which Israel had built, and then lost. But, as so often before, Jesus' intention is elsewhere. The greatness which he has to offer them goes beyond their expectations, but they are too satisfied with too much less.

Even the pharisee leaders enter the scene and make a comment (12:19) that shows the Johannine mind again: whether they like it or not, they are right—especially from the later perspective of the fourth evangelist—and his gentile church.

"The Hour has come!" (12:20-36)

We could wish that the evangelist had been more generous in telling his friends what he meant to suggest by introducing the Greeks (12:21), who come and disappear in a single verse, without ever engaging Jesus in a conversation. It may be that he intends to use this incident to show outsiders accepting Jesus with goodwill, in contrast to the unfaith of the pharisees and the other leaders (12:19). We have some other examples of this in the Fourth Gospel, in which the evangelist knows what he means to suggest, but he seems to take it for granted that the nuances which he gives will be clear enough (this seems to be the case, for example, in his description of John the Baptist in ch. 1, and of the Cana wedding incident in ch. 2).

In any case, these Greeks fade immediately into the background, and give way to Jesus and the last words of his Public Ministry. And these last words are so full of special themes that they go well with the

Lazarus incident, as a transition to the Great Passover which is about to begin (11:55; 12:1).

Whether Jesus addresses the Greeks or the disciples (12:23), is not entirely clear, but either way, he declares that "the hour" toward which he has been moving has finally arrived. He alluded to it for the first time in his brief dialogue with his mother at Cana (2:4), and he has mentioned it several times since, but always as something in the future. Now it is the time for his glorification, through his being "lifted up" in crucifixion and also in resurrection. The parable of the wheat grain (12:24-25) illustrates the theme of the "passover" from life to death and then on again to life. It is such an apt image that it also served Paul well, when he tried to explain the meaning of Jesus' resurrection to his philosophically-minded Greek converts (1 Cor 15:36-44). This is a new challenge to the imagination of those who hear Jesus' words—that death and the unknown should be preferable to the familiar experience of earthly life. Yet, Jesus insists by his hyperbole (v. 25) as well as by the verse which follows it, that this is the divine reality which he has come to bring about, not only for himself but also for those who are in his company. It is not enough for John's Christians to know who Jesus is and what he has done—they must walk the same path, and come to the same glory (v. 26)! Just as Jesus and the Father are one (10:30), likewise Jesus and his Church are one, and the Father will receive the servants in glory no less than he will receive the Son himself! All of this reminds us, in a brief way, of Paul's doctrine of the Church as the Mystical Body of Jesus, although Paul develops it much more fully (1 Cor 12; Ep 4 etc.) than the fourth evangelist does.

Verse 27 reveals another instance of Jesus' human side—which is rare in the Fourth Gospel—as he acknowledges the "trouble" that he feels. The word that the evangelist ascribes to Jesus here is the same as the one that he used in the scene at Bethany (11:33). The fourth evangelist does not describe Jesus' agony in Gethsemani, but here he shows what is practically an equivalent of it, if more briefly. His oneness with the Father must overcome his human reluctance, so that he can move on to what awaits him.

Jesus' brief dialogue with the Father shows that he is fully aware of who and what he is, and that in glorifying Jesus, the Father glorifies himself (v. 28-30). Surprising that the Father's reply to Jesus should be audible to the crowd, but, even though they are permitted to hear it and to know that it is a "voice" (v. 30), they remain outsiders to the dialogue itself. The content of it is not for them! Jesus is moving away from human communication, and from his earthly ministry, and preparing to return to his Father.

In the Johannine vocabulary "the world" is always humanity without God and without faith in Jesus' divine power to give God's life to men. In 3:17 the evangelist spoke of "the world" not to be judged but to be saved by the Son. But, since that conversation with the sophisticated but uncomprehending Nicodemus, Jesus has had little consolation from "the world"—not because it is evil—but because men have been bound by evil instead of being freed by Jesus (12:31). Now, however, this enslavement is to be ended, as Jesus is "lifted up" to be the gateway, leading all men through his death and passover, to the presence of the Father. John's Ephesian friends surely felt honored to know that "all men" (v. 32) included them, since they were members of a church that had moved away from its Jewish beginnings, to become truly universal!

The concluding stage of the dialogue is the final instance in the Public Ministry, of the crowd's inability to comprehend the level of Jesus' language. The Messiah is to remain forever, say the Scriptures (Ps 45:7; 89:5; Is 9:6; Dn 7:14); but the Son of Man is to be "lifted up" (12:34; 8:38), which usually means "taken up and away." His reply simply leaves them imprisoned in their own world of merely human logic and sense-understanding, which can never commune with the liberating divine realities. They still have the light with them, but not for long. The time of darkness—which this crowd seems to prefer—is near.

Retrospect and Summary (12:37-43)

The Book of Signs, which began in the first chapter of John's Gospel, is over. There has been a series of seven epiphanies, in which Jesus "manifested his glory" (2:11), and gave his disciples reason for believing in him. As he evaluates Jesus' Public Ministry now, the evangelist wonders how they could have missed the point so massively. There are precedents, however, as the Scriptures report. As a matter of fact, the whole history of the prophets is a history of rejected prophets. The first and second Isaiahs, whom the evangelist quotes here, had experienced the pain of being unbelieved and unaccepted. Isaiah's whole prophetic ministry had been inaugurated with a vision of God's glory (Is 6) and an assurance that he would meet unbelief. This is the pattern which is now evident also in the ministry of Jesus—and he had more to offer than Isaiah ever had. But, even though, like Nicodemus or the parents of the man cured of blindness, these crowds were not as hostile to Jesus as their leaders were, even so, they could not rise from the human level to the divine one. They could not see the glow of God in the face of Jesus! But the evangelist has made his picture clear enough, so that his friends in Ephesus should not make the same mistake. Their future glory depends on their being able to see what these people had sadly missed.

Questions for Consideration and Reflection

1. How do Jesus' own intentions and expectations show up in these chapters?
2. Why do we say that the incidents of these chapters are to prepare the Johannine church for "the hour?"
3. How do these chapters compare with the Synoptic Gospels?
4. What connection does the evangelist show here between Jesus and Isaiah?
5. What is the significance of the Greeks in chapter 12?
6. Is the evangelist unfair in his judgment of those who "refused to believe in him" (12:37)?

9

PARTING WORDS

"You are my friends, if you do what I command you" (Jn 15:14).

Preliminary Reading

Read Jn 13-17; allow yourself about an hour for this, reading the text slowly in order to absorb the mood. Try to imagine that you hear the various persons speaking, especially Jesus himself. Write your observations and comments as you read along. Notice especially the following features:

13:1 ". . . the hour had come for him to pass. . ."

14:16 ". . . he will give you another Paraclete. . ."

14:31 The original ending of the Last Supper Discourse;

15:20 The troubles that await Jesus' disciples;

17:20 Jesus prays for the present and future Church.

There is a familiar form that we find several times in both Testaments of the Bible, and that we can call the last remembered words of the departing leader. We have the last words of Jacob, Moses, Joshua, David, Isaiah, Jeremiah, Ezra and others, in the Old Testament. Here the fourth evangelist gives a lengthy discourse section that gives us Jesus' last remembered words to his disciples immediately before his return to the Father. In this way the Last Supper Discourse of the Fourth Gospel parallels the Eschatological Discourse, which has more prominence in the Synoptic Gospels (Mk 13; Mt 24-25; Lk 21), and which the Fourth Gospel does not have at all.

However, even before the discourse begins, the evangelist introduces the context. He has already spoken of Jesus' recent raising of Lazarus as the "last straw" which made Jesus a wanted man; now the leaders have decided to kill him. He has been anointed at Bethany and had his messianic entry into the capital. In all three of these events John has stressed that Jesus is really in control of the situation and that he is the only one who really understands what is happening, even though people around him think they know, but fail to comprehend the divine reality of it all.

Now the Book of Signs is finished, with its summary and verdict in 12:37-43. "They refused to believe . . . They preferred the praise of men to the glory of God." From this point on Jesus no longer offers himself or his ministry of words and signs to the crowds, or to "the Jews." This phase of his work is over and now, as the evangelist says at the beginning of the Book of Glory (13:1), the "hour" has come. This "hour" is not a sixty minute period; it is the time at which Jesus is to pass through suffering to glorification. John also describes this hour as the time set for Jesus to go over to the Father. The Book of Glory begins here, and this is the Johannine way of describing and interpreting Jesus' Passion and Death. It is his Glorification!

The Supper Setting (13:1-30)

The Last Supper scene has no eucharist because the eucharist section of the Fourth Gospel is contained in the sign of the loaves in chapter 6. Here the thing that dominates the supper scene is the atmosphere, and, along with it, the discourse. But before the discourse begins, we see a countersign of what Jesus is to do; there are three figures who, one way or another, appear as obstacles to Jesus, and in one way or another, Jesus overcomes these obstacles. The first is Satan. John presents him as a puppeteer, controlling poor Judas, who is the second figure. Luke makes the same point in his Gospel (Lk 22:3), and he may have gotten this idea from the teaching of the Beloved Disciple at Ephesus, since he certainly did not find it in Mark or Matthew. The third obstacle which Jesus overcomes is the incomprehension of Simon Peter. And Jesus overcomes Peter's failure to understand, simply by going ahead with his symbolic washing of the disciple's feet.

The foot washing occurs only in the Fourth Gospel, and is somewhat difficult to reconcile with the picture of Jesus as consistently divine and glorious, that the evangelist has maintained throughout his Gospel. Nevertheless, the scene is manifestly ecclesial, because it sets a standard for Peter and the others to follow in their relations, not with Jesus, but with each other: "as I have done, so you must do . . . you must wash each other's feet" (13:14-15). So this is not an example primarily of humility or of self-abasement, but of love and solicitude for others, of Jesus for the disciples, and of them for each other. Some commentators see here a subtle if secondary suggestion of baptismal washing, but it is difficult to say that this is the intention of Jesus here, or of the fourth evangelist either.

The ecclesial element is present also in the "new commandment" that Jesus gives them—the only commandment that he gives in the whole Fourth Gospel: "love one another, as I have loved you" (13:34). These are to be the hallmarks of the disciples: mutual love and mutual service, according to the example of the Lord. After his departure from their presence, these signs of his presence must remain among them.

Jesus shows that he knows what is going on: Judas must go about his task, and Jesus says again, "I AM!" (13:19), to show them that he claims divinity, even as he accepts and permits human betrayal. Judas goes, and John adds, simply but powerfully, "It was night" (13:30). This is irony too. Peter protests that he will follow Jesus wherever he goes, and Jesus shows again his divine knowledge of the situation. Peter will deny the Lord three times before the end of this night. This reminds us of what John said already in 2:23-25: he did not entrust himself to them . . . because he was well aware of human nature.

The Last Supper Discourse (13:31-17:26)

Now that he has set the narrative context, the evangelist moves on to present one of his most treasured passages, which his readers have cherished from that day to this—Jesus' Last Supper Discourse. We can well imagine how hard the ageing Beloved Disciple tried to give his Christian friends in Ephesus a memorable picture of the departing Lord and of the consoling and encouraging tone of the last words which he bequeathed to his disciples as his parting gift. Even here, as so often in the earlier incidents of the Gospel, the disciples repeatedly show their confusion. Peter, Thomas, Philip and Jude speak, and make this a dialogue, as they show by their brief interjections, that they are in a grey fog of uncomprehending goodwill, something like that of Nicodemus (ch. 3). With all of this as a framework, what Jesus really gives is, in effect, a monologue.

The core of the Last Supper Discourse is the first part (13:38-14:31); the rest consists of sayings of Jesus that were added here, perhaps by the evangelist, or more likely by a later editor. Throughout the discourse, we get the impression that the Apostle must have held his Christian followers spellbound, as he passed on to them the consoling and uplifting last words of the departing Lord. As he prepares to leave his disciples, Jesus stresses that he is one with them, and that they must be one with him and with each other, and with the Father, as he is. Jesus seems to be halfway between heaven and earth here, as he assures his chosen friends that, even though he is to leave them, they will see him again, and they will not be orphaned. What he asks of them is that they keep faith in him and in the Father, and keep the commandments that he has given them. But, surprisingly enough, as we have observed, John does not show Jesus enunciating a code of commandments; the only demand that Jesus makes of his disciples in the Fourth Gospel is "love one another as I have loved you" (13:34).

The rest of the Discourse is full of promise, encouragement and assurance. Jesus is to go, but the disciples will see him again—indeed they are to come to him and occupy the places that he will prepare for them in the Father's heavenly presence. We know that all three Synoptics present Jesus' prediction that he will be vindicated as Son of Man and return in a glorious *parousia*, to triumph over his former oppressors. But the Johannine message is different; Jesus does not speak in the Fourth Gospel of a future *parousia*, or second coming. His disciples will see him again not because he will return in a glorious triumph, but because he will show them his risen self, and then they will follow him in martyrdom, and come to join him in the fullness of resurrection-glory.

So they will come to the Father by following the way that Jesus is tracing out for them. It seems quite clear that the evangelist is here offering his Christian friends the prospect of following Jesus in the death of martyrdom; this is how they will come to see his glory for themselves.

Jesus also promises his disciples the gift of the Paraclete that the Father will send. This is a term which represents the forum of public legal affairs; a paraclete is an advocate or counselor, who stands alongside his clients when they are called to defend themselves in a public court. This paraclete is the spirit of truth, who will be their teacher. Even though the word "trinity" does not occur in the Fourth Gospel (or in the entire Bible, for that matter), we have here the seeds of the doctrine that will mature in the later centuries of the Church's theological understanding. Jesus does not explain fully who or what the Holy Spirit is, but he gives his disciples enough to prepare them for the transformation that will come over them after his death, when they will be made into dynamized apostles, instead of the frightened and confused disciples that they have been so far.

At the end of the original Discourse, in 14:27-31, Jesus appears not at all troubled or apprehensive. He says nothing about death or dying. He bids his friends the *shalom* peace greeting (14:27) which is the usual Jewish word of hello or goodbye. He makes a brief mention of the Prince of this world, but without any suggestion that Jesus has anything to fear from him. There is to be no real struggle between them, because there can be no real question of who is going to win.

This will simply be another illustration of what we saw in the Prologue, that the darkness cannot put out the light. But it is about to make a feeble try.

So Jesus is about to return to the Father—to be "lifted up." What a way to look at the whole thing! But this is the message of Saint John. It is only a blind eye that cannot see the divine reality in what is about to be acted through. This is why it is the Book of Glory! Jesus seems, not resigned to his fate, but eager to get started. He says, "Come, then, let us be on our way" (14:31).

These words of Jesus lead smoothly to the next narrative section, which begins in ch. 18. But before that, we have the additional material that has been added to amplify the Last Supper Discourse.

16:4b-33

If we pass on now to look immediately at 16:4b-33, we find a part of the Discourse that is practically a doublet of the first part. Jesus promises to send the Paraclete as the disciples' teacher and guide. He assures them that they will see him again, that he will come to them, and that he is now about to go to the Father. The disciples appear to be reassured and satisfied: "At last you are speaking plainly, without veiled language!" (16:29). Yet, they will soon make a poor showing as he is arrested and executed! It seems that they did not understand as well as they thought they did! More likely, they were just beginning to recognize the pattern of Jesus' words—but not really understanding them. They overestimate themselves, and for this reason Jesus is not at all reassured by their expression of satisfaction. He knows them too well, and he tells them so (16:32), just as he told Peter that he would weaken under pressure (13:38).

We notice the difference of atmosphere in these chapters. There are no disputes with unbelievers, no miracle-signs, no plots against Jesus. All is intimacy and gentleness. Jesus prepares his friends for a departure that he says will be good for them because it will bring them the Holy Spirit, and they will see him again besides! Although at first it might seem that this seeing him again is a prediction of his own resurrection, it is probably more than this. It is also a prediction of *their* resurrection as well, since they are to go along the same path as he is to take. The disciples surely do not understand this, because if they did, they would probably panic. Instead, they remain listening in rapt attention.

15:1-16:4a   When we move on to Jesus' words in this section, we see more of the same, with the familiar image of the vine and the branches. However, although the image is familiar from the Old Testament, there is a difference in the use of it here. In the OT, for example, in the vineyard song of Isaiah (Is 5) and also in the prophetic oracle of Jeremiah (Jr 2) the vineyard is Israel, but usually in a negative sense, insofar as Israel is the vine that fails to produce fruit, or that produces only bad fruit. However, there is a brief phrase in Ps 80:16-18, in which the psalmist calls himself the vine that God has planted and cared for. Sirach speaks later on, of divine wisdom sent out by God to dwell on earth, and budding forth delights like a vine (Si 24:17). All of these images appear fused together in John 15, as Jesus speaks of himself and his disciples as vine and branches. The image is different and innovative in the Fourth Gospel, but the message is the same as what Jesus has said before, and what the evangelist has already said in the Prologue. We have become accustomed to the symbolic quality of Johannine language; Jesus is *word, water, way, truth, life, sheepgate and shepherd,* so this image of *the vine and the branches* is quite in place here, even though it appears to be added to the original Discourse.

As Jesus moves on to tell the disciples, "live on in my love," (15:9), the terminology is remarkably similar to that of the first Johannine epistle. The apostolic message is also the same: an urgent exhortation to remain loyal to Jesus on the level of persevering love. The new commandment which recurs here (15:12), as he gave it in ch. 13, is both vertical and horizontal. The commandment to "love one another" is horizontal and ecclesial—remain close to each other; see me in each other; see each other living my life in union with the Father, taught and guided by the Holy Spirit whom I will send you from the Father. If you see this in each other, then you must love each other too, "as I have loved you." This means that Jesus demands of his disciples more than merely human affection; he demands the same self-giving-to-the-end that he is about to show them—free of the last possible dreg of self-love or self-seeking, for the good of others. This is the only commandment that Jesus leaves behind; this is the message of Saint John. And we know that this has consistenly been the principle that has animated the Church, the primacy of charity. We also know that it is a lifelong project to take this on and make it the driving principle of our lives. They tell the story of Saint John as an old man, so weak that he had to be carried. The only thing that he could do was sit and tell his disciples, "Little children love one another." We can see where he got the principle.

Clearly Jesus is preparing his disciples here for their ecclesial experience. He tells them things that they will need to remember after he is gone from them and before they see him again. This will be in the time of the Church—the time in-between; the realized final age has come, but it has not yet reached its final consummation. Along with the reassurance and challenge of these words Jesus also sobers the disciples by preparing them for the coming trials. "They will harry you as they have harried me" (15:20); "They will expel you from the synagogues . . . a time will come when anyone who kills you will claim to be serving God" (16:2). No doubt these things have already happened in the intervening years of John's apostolic experience. And he is not dismayed, because this is what Jesus said they would have to put up with. The pressure has come from unconverted Israelites, who no longer tolerate Jewish Christians in their assemblies (9:22; 12:42); and the martyrdom of Peter and Paul and the other members of the original band is already public history. John is also aware of the Roman pressures which are now bearing down on his friends. These words of Jesus which he draws from his store of precious memories, should animate and sustain them.

Chapter 17

The Priestly Prayer of Jesus in this chapter is different from the rest of the Discourse because these are words which Jesus addresses directly to the Father. They are also an expansion of the original Discourse, but they fit well into the context, despite some literary inconsistencies. We can imagine a luminous glow coming over Jesus here, as he gives audible expression to the intimacy of his union with the Father, and to the sentiments which fill his heart during his last earthly hours.

His concern is entirely for others; this is why we call this the Priestly Prayer, insofar as in it Jesus mediates on behalf of his followers, present and future. He is about to come back to the eternity which he left behind when he took on human flesh. Now his work is done, and well done at that. He is ready to resume the glory of the Father's divine presence, and the glory that he has allowed men to glimpse in his sign-miracles, for those who had the eyes of faith to see by. He takes a last glance at those whom he is about to leave behind, commending them to the Father as he entrusts to them the memory of his life-giving presence and his life-giving words. John no doubt has pondered these words of the now-absent Lord, and, like his ten colleagues who heard them with him on that night long ago, John has drawn unutterable joy from the fact that God's own Son prayed for them, and also for all who were to come to faith through their witness.

Here is another touch of the ecclesial task which Jesus entrusted to his disciples—to bring others to have faith. This is what John has done, and all of this is a call to them now, so that they may persevere in this faith even to the end, even to death under a Roman sword, if it should come to that. What a consolation these beleaguered Christians of Ephesus have felt when their venerable apostolic patriarch told them that the life-giving Lord, in his last earthly words, prayed for them to the timeless Father. And that the same absent Lord is waiting for them now, to join him, "in my company, where I am" (17:24). This is both consolation and promise. It must sustain them in the trial.

In recent years we have heard these words of Jesus, "That they may be one . . ." as a motto of the ecumenical movement among the various Christian churches. It is appropriate for that, because it is a constant reminder that this is the will of the Lord; it is also a reproach to the heirs of the apostolic faith that the tragedy of division has often prevented Christians from remembering—or following—the will of the absent Lord. So in this light, the Last Supper Discourse is not only consolation and promise, but it is also a challenge to all

Christians to be faithful to the Lord, not now in the face of Roman swords, or of Jewish ostracism, but in the face of a world that withholds its belief, waiting for Christians to practice what they say their Master preached.

Questions for Consideration and Reflection

1. How does this Last Supper section compare with the Last Supper sections of the Synoptic Gospels?
2. What does the evangelist say here about the eucharist? Why?
3. For what does Jesus appear to be preparing his disciples?
4. Why do commentators say that chapter 13 begins the "Book of Glory?" Is this a correct description of chapters 13-21?
5. What reaction does John seem to be trying to arouse in his disciples, as he repeats these words of Jesus?
6. How does the evangelist's message in these chapters compare with the message of 1 John?

10

THE ROYAL ROAD TO GLORY

"When Jesus took the wine, he said, 'Now it is finished.' Then he bowed his head, and delivered over his spirit" (Jn 19:30).

Preliminary Reading

Read Jn 18-21. Allow yourself about an hour to an hour and a half for this. Try to imagine the effect that the evangelist is trying to have on his readers (or hearers). Write down your observations, and notice the significance of these details:

18:10 The name of the slave whom Jesus heals;

19:2   The trappings of royalty;

19:22 Pilate's refusal to change the text of the inscription;

19:25 Mary at Calvary;

20:22 The Risen Lord confers the Holy Spirit on the disciples.

We have already observed that the Last Supper Discourse is a unique contribution of the fourth evangelist, with no corresponding parallel in the Synoptic Gospels. We have also seen that he begins the Book of Glory with 13:1, and the comment that Jesus knew that his "hour" had arrived and it was now time for him to be "lifted up" both in crucifixion-death and in resurrection-glory. With all these theological suggestions generously distributed for the benefit of his readers (or hearers, if we consider that the Gospel was meant to be listened to, rather than read), our evangelist has now only to describe Jesus' actual carrying through of these themes. This is why we say that these chapters (13-21), which could appear so sad and tragic, really constitute the "Book of Glory." They are the Johannine description, not of Jesus' failure in his mission and his pathetic acceptance of the role of the Suffering Servant of God, but to the eyes of faith, to which John constantly appeals, they are the picture of Jesus' triumphal procession to Calvary, which is the place of his royal enthronement. From there Jesus takes his final departure from the earthly condition which he has shared with men, and his return to the divine glory which was really his all the while, and which he has never really given up.

It is not very difficult to imagine the Apostle being asked time and again, by unconverted Jews, by new Christians, or even by interested pagans, "How can you expect us to see divine glory in an executed convict?" John's answer is here in these last chapters of his Gospel. We can also imagine the sense of urgency that presses upon to give to his Christian friends a response that will be both convincing and inspiring. If he fails to give them such a response, he can hardly expect them to persevere in Christian faith, much less to accept the inevitability of execution in punishment for rejecting the Roman emperor's demand for a divine salute.

We recognize, of course, the underlying unity of the Passion History, which this teacher shares with the other evangelists. Yet, the special Johannine touch is in just about every verse of these chapters. The pause and falling back of the arresting soldiers; Jesus' insistence that the disciples should not be arrested; the name of Malchus; the lengthy interviews with Annas and Pilate; the presence of Jesus' mother at Calvary; the special prominence of the Beloved Disciple—

all of these features, which we find only in this Gospel, show the independence and the particularly personal reminiscences which the fourth evangelist contributes to the Gospel of Jesus' glorification.

Arrest

Right at the beginning we see another subtle twist of the Johannine irony that has become a familiar feature of the Fourth Gospel. The soldiers are looking for "Jesus of Nazareth." But Jesus answers, "I AM!" He has used this phrase before, to identify himself with Jahweh, the God of Israel! Not even Peter gets the point here, because if he had gotten it, he would hardly have been so brash as to pull a sword and try to prevent the whole thing from happening! Caiaphas appears only in passing (18:13), but even so, he adds to the irony (as he did earlier in 11:51-52), by saying exactly the right thing, but for the wrong reason—and not realizing in the slightest that he was doing it—prophesying that one man must die for the people.

The Participants

All these individual persons who have a part in the Passion Gospel, come and go, like the servants who hear Peter's confused and frightened denial of Jesus at cock-crow time, and like Annas and his servants. They fill in the background scenes, as they lead up to the governor, Pontius Pilate, who is one of the great tragic figures of all human history, unredeemed and unrehabilitated for all time, like Judas. This self-serving puppet governor of an obscure backwater province of the Roman empire, struts and postures like a petty king, in the presence of the Word made flesh. Jesus simply refuses to accommodate him; he shows neither the servility of one who hopes for mercy, nor the toughness of a hardened criminal. The dialogue between the two of them represents a private interview, like the one with Nicodemus. The topic, of all things, is kingship! We would have to look far and wide to find an abyss wider than the one which separates Pilate's mind from that of Jesus! The key words of the

interview are *king* and *truth* (18:33-39). These are two realities that
Pilate simply cannot handle. So he bluffs, and Jesus lets it all happen.
The same for the cloak of royal purple, and the crown (19:2); these are
intended to be cruel jokes, but the joke is really not on Jesus! He is on
the royal way of return to the Father, marching head and shoulders
above the human blindness that surrounds him!

Calvary

Perhaps the supreme irony of the Passion Gospel is the section
about the inscription on the cross, written in three languages,
incidentally, to add to the intensity of the scene. Poor Pilate refuses to
change the text as the priests demand, because that would be
equivalent to admitting that he has made a mistake—and rather than
do that, he gives his famous reply, "What I have written, I have
written" (19:22), thereby declaring for all time the very truth that he
had no intention of recognizing!

Only the fourth evangelist shows Mary at Calvary (19:25-27); he
calls her the "mother of Jesus" here, as he did when she was at the
Cana wedding. How many artists and preachers have interpreted this
scene, over the centuries! John surely had another of his precious
memories here—the memory of the years that he had had, to cherish
her presence with him, after the Lord's departure. And after their own
move from Palestine, when they lived in Ephesus, she was the most
precious treasure of the young church there—the bringer of God.
There is a level of symbolic suggestion here, which surpasses the
immediate level of the narrative. As the woman of faith, Mary is a
microcosm of the people of God, the Church, now entrusted to the
care of the Disciple by the departing Lord. Together, then, these two
now represent the Church which Jesus at his departure has entrusted
to the care of the apostles—to cherish, comfort, maintain, as John
was to do for Mary.

Even the moment of Jesus' death comes across in the Fourth
Gospel as a moment full of powerful significance. There is no
earthquake, no splitting of the Temple veil, no darkness at noon, no
centurion crying out, as there are in the Synoptic Gospels. But there is

Jesus' own word of satisfaction, as he sighs and says, "It is finished"
(19:30), and gives up, or delivers over, his spirit. This phrase, "giving
up the ghost," can mean simply that he died. But there is a school of
thought that sees here a subtle Johannine hint, suggesting that Jesus,
by his dying breath, actually passes on to the Church the Holy Spirit,
as he promised to his disciples in the Last Supper Discourse. We can
see the same subtlety in the blood and water which flow from Jesus'
side after the soldier thrusts the lance. John quotes from the
Scripture—"Break none of its bones"—referring to the lamb which
the Jews ate at the Passover celebration (Ex 12:46). But beyond this
obvious suggestion there is the deeper symbolism of the blood and
water, both symbols of life, which come from the body of the dying
Lord. The death of the lamb gives life. And even beyond this, some
commentators see a level of sacramentalism in the blood and water,
suggesting baptism and eucharist. But, with all the symbolism and
suggestion, there is no possible doubt that Jesus is dead. Pierced and
drained, now devoid even of life-breath, he has loved to the end, and
given to the Father the fullness of his loyalty, conceding nothing to
the malice that now can do no more to him. Yet there is not the
lightest trace of defeat or tragedy here. All of this has simply fitted
together as his return to the Father. Now that he has been lifted up, he
is glorified, divinely triumphant, basking in the radiance of the
Father's presence, approved, appreciated and loved by him.

Easter

When the evangelist moves on to the next chapter to speak of the
Risen Lord, he has a slant that is different again from the view of the
Synoptics. In all three of the Synoptic Gospels and in the early
kerygmatic preaching of Peter and of the other apostles which Luke
has summarized in the *Acts of the Apostles*, the pattern of the Paschal
Mystery is one of reversal, as humiliation is followed by exaltation.
We call this, in theological terms, the combination of low and high
Christology, reflecting the Old Testament themes of the Son of Man
and the Suffering Servant. But John's Christology is, as we have said,
consistently high. Jesus is always the Word and the Son, ever at the

Father's side (1:18). This is why we say that there is no defeat or tragedy for Jesus in the Fourth Gospel. There is no fight to the death between good and evil, because there was never any other way that it could go, but for God and good to be eternally above evil and death. There is defeat and tragedy here, but not for Jesus; it is rather the failure of those whose blindness prevents them from relating to the divine reality that is operative here. Our evangelist said in 13:1, at the beginning of the Book of Glory, that "the hour" had come for Jesus to pass over from this world to the Father. This is what he has now done. So, instead of showing a reversal of his lowly state to a high state, the Johannine picture shows the various clues of Jesus' royalty and his perfect control of the situation, as he allows men to follow freely their own sinfulness and blindness, thereby manifesting the supremacy of the Father who now receives him in glory.

It follows from this that the Risen Lord who presents himself to the disciples after Calvary is not different from the Glorious Lord who was made flesh and worked the signs, who said repeatedly, "I AM!" John has preserved the early apostolic tradition of the disciples' Easter experience—the woman, the empty tomb, the apparitions. But there is no reversal of Jesus' situation here; there is only the confirmation of what he said, the manifestation of his glorified and risen self, as he really is and as he was before—as he lets himself be seen now, by the few whom he has chosen to be his witnesses to the rest of the world.

There is no question here that Jesus lives and is risen; Mary sees the empty tomb and runs in panic, without understanding. Peter and the other Disciple come running; they see the empty tomb, and the burial clothes neatly folded (20:7), not disheveled as they would be if the body had been hastily stolen. But here again, there is a twofold point: none of them had known what to expect, because none of them had understood the Scriptures about the third day, the Son of Man, the Suffering Servant etc. Neither had they understood Jesus' words when he told them of himself in these terms. What they came to see and know, was not something that they were expecting, or something that they had figured out for themselves. It was something that was revealed to them from beyond themselves. And it leaves them dismayed!

The other point is the comparison of Peter and the other Disciple (who is evidently John). Peter's denial of Jesus was a failure to witness to the Lord, and it has cost him something. The other Disciple respects him, waits for him, lets him go in first. Peter enters, observes, notices the cloths. But it is the younger Disciple, the patriarch of the Ephesian church now, who gets the credit for seeing and believing. Peter has not been cast off, but he has fallen; it is a wonder that he is allowed to come to the tomb at all. But, even so, his later work as leader of the Church is no less a fact of history than his denial of the suffering Lord. The credit ultimately goes not to Peter, but to the rehabilitating and forgiving Lord, who had a plan for Simon, as he had shown in their first encounter (1:42), when he changed his name to Kephas.

The same comparison will show up again in the Appendix to the Gospel, in chapter 21. The scene there is Galilee, and the disciples are fishing. Peter has no eminence here, no first place among the brethren; he is simply one of the fishermen. And when Jesus presents himself, Peter is ashamed and embarrassed, but it is given to the Beloved Disciple to recognize that, "It is the Lord!" (21:7).

When we come to the scene of Mary Magdalene weeping at the tomb (20:11 ff.)—the tomb that she does not even have the courage or the presence of mind to enter—we wonder whether the evangelist has a smile on his face as he recounts this to his friends. No wonder she could not understand or recognize—how could she allow herself to weep at a time like this? Do we cry and mourn when we see a king crowned and throned, radiant in royal splendor? Mary's weakness is that she is so human. But her humanity covers her eyes. She cannot pierce the darkness as the Beloved Disciple did; and when the Risen Lord shows himself, she is still so human that she needs another gentle prodding, which Jesus gives here by speaking her name (20:16). And still then, she is so human that even when she does come to recognize him, she clings to his feet, as if to hold him for herself. But the Risen Lord is still in control of himself and of the situation. She must not cling, or try to hold him back. This apparition is a gift to her, but not for her alone. She must let him be what he really is, not on her merely human terms, but on his divine terms; he is to complete his return to the Father, which he has interrupted momentarily, so to speak, between the tomb and the Father's presence, in order to pause and console her in her grief, by giving her a glimpse of his splendor. Now that she knows, she too must witness by telling the others—those who will be Jesus' brothers now because they share his life of Sonship by faith—that he lives, and has gone to the God who is their God as well as his, because he has called them to be with him, and shown himself to them.

Thomas' mistake is basically the same as Mary's (20:24 ff.); he wants to know Jesus in a human way, by enjoying the consolation of touching his risen flesh. And Jesus makes a concession to him too, as he did to Mary. And why not? Accepting Thomas' touch is no more of a chore for the Risen Lord than coming into a room in spite of a locked door! The atmosphere of these apparitions is characterized by unspeakable joy and peace—the *shalom* of a friendly hello. And there is the mission. The Risen Lord is not for them alone; they must witness now, and sanctify others, liberating and purifying men from sin. For Thomas, who was so human and so stubborn, there is a word of gentle rebuke, from a Lord who seems to smile at this well intentioned blundering. The evangelist makes capital of the Risen Lord's rebuke to Thomas, because this is the same message as the one that he must give to his followers in Ephesus: Christians have to persevere and keep faith in the same Risen Lord, not on the strength of what they have seen or touched of his risen flesh, but on the word of apostolic witness, which underpins the Church.

Thomas' response is even fuller and more complete than Mary's intimate and very feminine "Rabbouni!" and more of what an apostle should be ready to declare. There is no more need for signs or words and works for Thomas. He has had all that he needs, and now he can say what the whole Church must say after him—and what Jesus told him long before that he was—Lord and God, in human form, but glorified, numinous, subtle, live-giving and divine. There may be a smile on the evangelist's face here also, especially as he repeats to his followers Jesus' words to Thomas. But, at least one way or the other, Thomas has gotten the message, and this brings him a long way beyond the obtuseness that burdened him before.

The Conclusion (21:24-25)

John's Gospel originally was to conclude with the final remarks in 20:30-31, before a later editor added the last chapter as an Appendix. So this new conclusion (21:24-25) is really a summary of the whole Gospel, and at the same time it is a guide for whatever future lies ahead for the Johannine church. If they are to have life in Jesus' name, and follow him to glory by the same path as the one that he took, then a backward glance at all that John has shown them should suffice to point them to where they are to go. The signs—and there are others as well, tell the tale, and manifest the glory, the glow of God's presence, in human visibility. They make faith worthwhile—worth having and worth keeping.

Questions for Consideration and Reflection

1. Is the evangelist successful in presenting Jesus' passion as his glorification? How?
2. What examples of Johannine irony do we find in these chapters?
3. Is the divinity of Jesus evident in these chapters?
4. What is the symbolic value of the blood and water of 19:34; of Mary's presence at Calvary (19:25-27); of the Beloved Disciple's remark in 21:7?
5. Is the conclusion to the Gospel (20:30-31) adequate? Why?

11

APOCALYPTIC AND REVELATION

"This is the revelation God gave to Jesus Christ, that he might show his servants what must happen very soon. He made it known by sending his angel to his servant John . . ."(Rv 1:1).

Preliminary Reading

Read through the entire *Book of Revelation*, preferably at one sitting. Allow yourself about an hour to an hour and a half for this. Do not allow yourself to be discouraged by the unfamiliar or obscure style of the language. Instead, concentrate on seeing the basic pattern of dualism in the conflict between the Christian Church and the pagan oppressors, and the assurance of eventual victory for the Church. Notice also the "apocalyptic" style itself, whereby the "seer" receives a message from the glorified Jesus, and transmits it to his Christian contemporaries.

A. The Style

The *Book of Revelation* (or the *Apocalypse*, as it was called in some earlier English versions) usually gets very little attention from contemporary Bible readers. Sometimes people say, "I tried it, but it was so confusing that I couldn't get anything out of it." This is not surprising, since the entire book is composed in a form of language that is replete with exotic symbolism and fantastic imagery; and these are alien to the style of writing—religious or otherwise—which people are likely to understand or appreciate nowadays.

There is a good deal of this apocalyptic style in many other books of the Bible too. If we want to absorb the message and the lessons which these ancient writers intended to present, then, rather than forfeit a large part of the Scriptures, we need instead to build for ourselves at least a minimal understanding of the basic features of this literary form. Even though we must admit that much of the symbolism escapes us nowadays, nevertheless, with some preliminary study as background, we can begin to grasp the fundamentals of apocalyptic language, and build up from there.

Continuity with the Past

There is a connection between the later apocalyptic writers of the Old Testament, and the ancient prophets of Israel who preceded them. Even though there is a notable difference in the style of their language, there is a basic unity in their messages. The earlier prophets, beginning with Moses and continuing with Samuel, Isaiah, Jeremiah and others, received God's self-revelation in the form of "the word of God" and passed it on to their contemporaries. In various ways they recognized God revealing himself and his plan in the historical events of their own day, and called on their people to follow and serve this one God instead of the many gods of their pagan neighbors. Right up to the time of the Babylonian exile (587 B.C.), the line of prophetic preachers in Israel is constant over the course of about seven centuries, with Moses remaining the prototype and standard of all legitimate prophecy.

Influences From Outside Israel

There seems to be a definite influence which came into Israel from Persia, about the time of the great exile and afterwards. This was the time of the new Zoroastrian religious movement in Persia, and even though many Jews returned to Palestine after the captivity in Babylonia, the Persian culture affected them, both in Palestine itself and in the wider world outside, which came to be influenced by Persian culture until it was countered by that of Greece less than two centuries later. The Persians had a special interest in astral cults and symbolic imagery, and a basic religious dualism which considered the two principles of good and evil, or light and darkness, to be locked in an endless conflict.

It seems that this style of language began to come into the speech and literature of the later prophets of Israel, beginning with Ezekiel, who lived among the exiles in Babylonia and shows many traces of this style in his oracles. In this the later prophets merely followed the example of the earlier Israelites, who had borrowed and imitated the terminology of their neighbors, except that in the earlier period the influences came principally from the Egyptians, and even more from the Canaanites and their fertility cult. The history of Israel in the entire Old Testament period shows constant borrowing by the Israelites from the cultures of other peoples—for better or worse, since these borrowings often led them to imitate pagan practices and compromise their own religious identity. Oddly enough, the apocalyptic writers of Israel eventually adapted this foreign style of language, precisely to defend and preserve Israel's religious identity when it was being threatened by foreign influences.

Israelite Adaptations

But imitating a foreign style of speaking and writing is not the same as absorbing a foreign religion. So, during and after the great exile, while the principal prophets became remembered as preachers of the word of God from an increasingly remote past, preachers of a new type gradually emerged. These were the "seers," whose message was related to the preaching of the earlier prophets, but whose style of language was very different. We see this, for example, in the "pre-apocalyptic" books of Ezekiel (chs. 1-3; 38-39), Zechariah (chs. 1-6) and Joel (chs. 1-4). Since the real flowering of apocalyptic in Israel came only later, we call these "seers" and their "visions" pre-apocalyptic, to distinguish them from the real apocalyptists, who wrote from about 200 B.C. to 100 A.D.

In these chapters we see the old prophetic preaching presented in a new form. The message shows the same holy zeal and jealous Jahwist monotheism of the earlier prophets, but these later books emphasize the medium of "visions" which bring a revelation from God to his people, through the meditation of the "seer." The Greek word *apocalypsis* means "revelation," and this is why the term describes this kind of message; the "seer" receives the revelation from God in a vision, and then he passes it on to his people. With regard to the visions, the preachers are "seers;" with regard to transmitting God's message to their contemporaries, they follow in the line of the ancient prophets like Moses.

Features of Apocalyptic Language

Apocalyptic as a message always come to people who are suffering persecution, in order to assure them that God will soon intervene on their behalf, overcome their oppressors, and inaugurate a new age of peace for those who persevere in faith in spite of foreign pressure. This conflict of persecuted faithful and foreign oppressors is the basis of the dualism which is a constant feature of apocalyptic. But here the dualism is principally institutional, contrasting two opposing groups of people, rather than the moral dualism which we have seen in 1 Jn and in the Gospel According to John (the contrast of good and evil, light and darkness etc.).

The other basic feature of apocalyptic we may call "promise" or, more technically, "eschatology." The seer looks ahead to assure his people that the troubles of the present time are really under God's control and permitted by him. When he is ready, God will intervene, defeat his enemies (and those of his faithful servants) in a definitive conflict, and reward his own people for their perseverance, by bringing them to an era of unimaginable joy and blessing. We see elements of this pattern in the "pre-apocalyptic" visions which we mentioned above. However, it is only occasional at this stage, whereas later on this style of language becomes widespread, even commonplace, among Jews and Jewish Christians.

In addition to these basic features of the apocalyptic message, there are a number of secondary features, which are mostly elements of style. These include the device of describing fantastic visions; monstrous beasts; good and evil demons or spirits (angels and devils); massive battles fought in the heavens, or on the clouds; God's lordship described in terms of a heavenly throne-room; mysterious numbers; upheavals and disturbances in the course of nature, etc. We need to bear in mind that these are elements of style and features of the apocalyptic language, so that we can avoid the mistake of taking them too literally, and confusing the medium with the message!

The "Apocalyptic" Period

In the early years of the second century B.C., the Greeks and Syrians encroached more and more on the cultural and religious life of the post-exilic Israelite people. Eventually a full-scale religious persecution was underway, designed to eliminate the Jahweh religion entirely and replace it with Greek-style polytheism. The Maccabees resisted on the military level, by their guerrilla-type defensive war, which succeeded in recapturing Jerusalem and restoring (at least for about a generation) Israel's autonomy as a nation. It was also at this time that the writer of the Book of Daniel brought a renewal of prophecy, by presenting to his Jewish contemporaries the stories and visions of the ancient hero in apocalyptic form. Thus the Book of Daniel is "resistance literature," which is basically a message of consolation and encouragement. It combines the scenes of Daniel and his dealings with the various Babylonian kings (chs. 1-6), with the exotic and bizarre visions of the future age (chs 7-12). These latter chapters are the real apocalyptic parts of the book, which contain all the basic features of this style. They bring a message which calls upon the beleaguered Jews to keep their faith under foreign persecution as Daniel and his friends did in the old days, and assuring them that God will intervene and save them too, as he saved Daniel and his friends in the past.

Soon after this, the Roman period began, and this is the background against which the apocalyptic style continued to circulate among Jews, and eventually among the early Christians as well. It appears in the Synoptic Gospels (e.g. Mk 13; Mt 27:45-53 etc.) and in some of Saint Paul's letters (1 Th 4:13 ff.; 2 Th 2:12 etc.). Now, at the end of the first century A.D., it appears full-blown in distinctively Christian form, in the whole Book of Revelation. The Christian form of apocalyptic draws from the earlier form, but now the dualism represents the conflict between the Roman empire and the Christian Church. The "promise" is an assurance that an era of peace awaits faithful Christians (especially the martyrs) in the future. However, there is a major difference now between the Jewish apocalyptic of the Old Testament, and the new Christian form. According to the Old Testament apocalyptic "seers," the promised future era was to be a time of earthly peace and prosperity, but, for the new Christian Church, in the light of the death and glorification of Jesus, the Christian eschatological promise offers eternal life with God in heaven, to Christians who remain faithful to Jesus even to the extent of enduring death by martyrdom.

There are other examples of this kind of literature, among the non-biblical writings, such as the Dead Sea Scrolls of Qumran, the *Fourth Book of Esdras* etc. Even the early Christian writers continued to speak to their fellow Christians in this kind of language, until about the beginning of the second century A.D., as we see in such writings as the *Apocalypse of Peter*, the *Apocalypse of Paul* etc. However, these works were not known to come from the Apostles, and they were never included in the Bible. They are among the collection of non-biblical writings called "New Testament (or Christian) Apocrypha."

B. In the Johannine Church

It is so obvious that the Book of Revelation is entirely different in

style and tone from both the Gospel According to John and the First
Epistle of John, that we can see why most commentators nowadays
agree that the author of Revelation was not the author of the other
Johannine writings. The early Christian tradition ascribed all of these
writings to the Beloved Disciple, but, as we have seen, we can
recognize the Apostle as the teacher behind these writings without
necessarily seeing him as the writer who put out the documents. The
fact that the seer calls himself "I, John" in the first and last chapters of
Revelation, makes us think of the Apostle, but it could well be
another man of the same name. If the writer was the Apostle, we
would expect him to identify himself by using his uniquely privileged
title. He surely was Jewish, because he has such a command of the
apocalyptic style and of the Old Testament Scriptures, which he
quotes continually, that biblical images and terminology flow from
him with unconscious ease. Also, there are theological similarities
which associate Revelation with the other Johannine literature in
spite of the differences in the literary form. So we can feel sure of our
ground if we follow the opinion of those who hold that the author of
Revelation was a Jewish member of the Johannine church, who
wrote his work about 95 A.D., after the death of Saint John the
Apostle.

The apocalyptic style, which was originally a Jewish form of
prophecy, has come now to have a Christian meaning. This is why the
dualism of Revelation represents the conflict between the Christian
Church and its enemies, particularly the Roman empire and its
emperor Domitian (81-96 A.D.), who drew Christian opposition to
himself when he demanded that his subjects greet him as a god. As for
the promise of eventual relief and future glory for those who
persevere in faith under the pressure of foreign persecution, the future
glory is now future heavenly glory; this will be the reward of those
who remain faithful, even if they must accept death by martyrdom at
the hands of the Roman pagans. The basic Old Testament lines are
still present, but the old apocalyptic language has been adapted to the
new Christian reality. The one who sends the message (the
"revelation" of the "apocalypse") is the risen and glorified Jesus, and
the seer who transmits it to his friends is the follower of the Beloved

Disciple who uses this symbolic language to encourage his troubled Christian contemporaries.

Structure of the Book

Some commentators think that Revelation is made up of at least three documents which were originally separate and eventually fused into one. This explanation helps us to understand the somewhat jumbled order of the contents, and the frequent repetitions of the main theme. We cannot be completely sure that this explanation is correct, but it is a respectable opinion which makes good sense.

In any case, we notice, after the opening verses of the Introduction (1:1-3), the section with the seven letters to the seven churches (1:4-3:22). Then come two septets: first of all the tableau of the seven seals (4:1-8:1), and then the one with the seven trumpets (8:2-11:19). The next section (chs. 12-14) contains a series of the seer's visions, of the Dragon and the Woman; the Dragon and Michael; the two Beasts; the Lamb and his Champions; the Three Angels and the Final Harvest. After these there is another septet in chs. 15-16; this time there are seven bowls, containing seven plagues which will be poured out on the earth. The remaining chapters (17:1-22:5) show visions of the end of the world, the defeat and destruction of the enemies (depicted as beasts) and the future heavenly reward of the faithful Christians. The last few verses (22:6-21) are an epilogue which draws the whole book to its conclusion.

We must be modest in our expectations, and realistic enough to admit that much of this terminology is not intelligible to us now, and that we cannot be sure what the "seer" meant by every detail. But we can figure out the basic message and we can see the Old Testament background which underlies many of the images. We can also read "between the lines" and figure out some aspects of the "seer's contemporary situation. If we approach it as a challenge to our literary imagination and our theological interest, we can take up these sections one at a time, and we can be sure that after we finish the project, we will know more about the Book of Revelation than we did when we started it, and perhaps more than we thought we would at all.

12

THE SEPTETS

"The Lamb that was sacrificed is worthy to be given power, riches, wisdom, strength, honor, glory and blessing" (Rv 5:12).

Preliminary Reading

Read Rv 1-11. Try to concentrate on the basic patterns which recur. Try also to grasp the message which the "seer" presents to his own contemporaries in those scenes. Notice especially the following details:
1. The principal sections:
    Prologue (1:1-3)
    The Seven Letters (1:3-3:22)
    The Seven Seals (4:1-8:1)
    The Seven Trumpets (8:2-11:19);
2. The frequent use of "sevens;"
3. The similarity of the septets of the seals and of the trumpets;
4. The prominence of the martyrs;
5. The call for endurance in trial.

A. The Seer's Prologue (1:1-3)

Strictly speaking, the first few verses of Revelation are not so much an introduction to the seven letters which follow immediately; rather, they are a Prologue which calls attention to the important "prophetic message" of the entire Book of Revelation, and to the things that are about to happen. We notice at once how this differs from both First John and the Fourth Gospel; both of these remember the past (the earthly work of Jesus), and apply it to the faith-life of the disciples in the later generation. However, this message, like apocalypse in general, looks more to the future which God has in store beyond the present.

Another thing that comes through in this Prologue is the "chain of command." Ultimately, the message comes from God (the Father), who has made Jesus his messenger to mankind. (This reminds us of the Prologue of the Fourth Gospel). Jesus and God the Father then appoint John to be the prophet, or the seer, who has the task of reporting this divine message to his fellow Christians, so that their spirits may be uplifted as they learn what the future holds for them, in spite of their present trials. There seems to be a certain urgency about it, since the seer says "very soon" (v. 1), and "the appointed time is near!" (v. 3). When we realize the pressures which burdened the Christians of Ephesus in the mid-90s of the first Christian century, we can see that they would certainly need and appreciate a prophetic assurance that their troubles would soon be over. However, "soon" is a vague word, and we come to see eventually that, though the Church has the assurance of ultimate victory and peace, the message for the present time is basically a call to endurance and perseverance in faith under pressure.

B. The Seven Letters (1:4-3:22)

Some commentators say that this section, with the seven letters to the seven churches, was not a part of the original message of the seer, but that it was added only later to the other chapters of Revelation. True enough, there are some similarities with the rest of the book, both in the apocalyptic style and in the content of the message; also, the seer identifies himself in 1:4 and 1:9, so that he seems to be the same as the John who presents the Prologue (1:1-3) and as the one who draws the book to its conclusion in the Epilogue (22:8). This gives a unity to these parts, at least insofar as they all come from the same John (although, as we have seen, this John is probably a member of the Johannine church of Ephesus, but not the Apostle who has the same name).

Nevertheless, the section of the seven letters stands apart, in several ways, from the rest of Revelation. So we are probably on solid ground if we hold that the letters were originally a separate booklet produced by the same person as the one who produced the rest of the work, and that even the rest of Revelation was originally two separate booklets. All three of these smaller booklets were eventually combined by the same John. This explains how and why there are differences, and also why the septet of the letters shows the same hand as the later chapters show.

If we look at a map of the biblical world, we can find the seven churches of the Apocalypse easily enough. Some people who have traveled as tourists or pilgrims, cherish the memory of their experience in visiting modern Turkey, and in seeing what remains of these biblical places now. They are all in western Turkey, rather close to the Aegean Sea (although they are not all on the coast). The island of Patmos, where the seer first received the message and the mission of transmitting it, is in the Aegean, only about 100 km. from Ephesus. Laodicea, Colossae and Ephesus are related also to Saint Paul in various ways, as we see from his letters, and also from the Acts of the Apostles.

It is quite obvious that the seer (John) was Jewish, because his language is so full of references to the Old Testament (especially to Ezekiel, Zechariah and Daniel), that he shows himself to be thoroughly familiar with the Old Testament books. Yet, he is also obviously Christian, since he transforms the imagery of these ancient Scriptures to fit the situation of the Christians of his own day. Whereas God was the author of the message in the Old Testament books under the name of Jahweh, here the one who presents himself to the seer is the Risen and Glorious Jesus, the "son of Man," as Jesus often called himself, using the imagery of Daniel (ch. 7). The whole description of Jesus is addressed, in typically apocalyptic style, to the lively imagination of the people who hear this message read to them. It defies logic, but it makes an impression on the fantasy. Jesus comes across here as divine, resurrected from death, having all power and knowledge, the master of heaven, earth, and the underworld (i.e. death) as well. Through the maze of Old Testament terminology and imagery, and with the symbolism of totality which the number seven represents, the pattern of the message for this section emerges: the Lord Jesus commissions John the seer, to transmit a message to seven Christian communities.

Then come the seven letters. Unfortunately, we cannot recognize all of the details which we find indicated in the letters, because we do not know the fine points of the situation in each of these local churches at the seer's time. But we can see that all seven of the letters have some things in common. The whole communication is on the level of spirit, since each letter is addressed to a "presiding spirit," or to an "angel," and each letter concludes with an urgent call to heed "the Spirit's word" (the divine authority of Jesus seems to be identical here with that of "the Spirit").

The messages themselves in the letters are a combination of praise and rebuke. Most churches get a measure of each, but Sardis and Laodicea come off looking especially bad, since they get the strongest rebukes and the most severe warnings to repent. Again, the symbolic character of the language clouds the message somewhat, so that we have to be satisfied with a minimal picture of the situation, even though we would like to have more detail. The praise and credit are for the fidelity and perseverance that these Christian groups are maintaining in the face of pressure and persecution, apparently from both Jews and pagans. The traumatic failure of the Jewish revolt of 66-70 A.D. had brought on the destruction of Jerusalem by Titus' Roman legionnaires, and since that tragic event, the tension between Jews and Christians had become more of a definitive break. Mutual hostility followed, and the Johannine church of Ephesus apparently had a strong measure of this to contend with, as well as the attractions of the Greek and Roman idol cults, and the newly-growing emperor cult.

The element of blame and rebuke which we see in the letters suggests that the original enthusiasm of these new converts has begun to wane. There has been backsliding, with too many concessions to corrosive members and to tendencies which compromise with non-Christian lifestyles, instead of breaking with them completely. The mysterious Nicolaitans appear by name in the letters to Ephesus and Pergamum, but we are not sure entirely just what their sin is. The chief sin of these young churches is a cooling of their zeal and of their first fervor in faith, and especially in their charity. They must regain this intensity of faith, avoid the harmful influences which come from within their membership, and endure patiently the tribulations which come from outsiders. The reward for this will be heaven, which the seer describes by several symbols, such as "the tree of life" (2:7), escaping the "second death" (i.e. hell) in 2:11, and being inscribed in the "book of the living" (3:5).

C. The Septet of the Seals (4:1-8:1)

It can be helpful for us if we compare the septet of the seals with the septet of the trumpets (8:2-11:19). Both of these septets have basically the same structure. Both are four chapters long. Both emphasize the number seven, which is a favorite symbol of totality and perfection—and in this case the sevens represent the totality of all creation that is under the control of God (both good and evil). Each of these two septets has an impressive (if fantastic) opening scene, in which the seer is brought to see the splendor of God's heavenly throne-room with his surrounding ministers, and to know the plan which God has decreed for all his creatures. When the seer comes to know God's plan this way, he learns that it includes the troubles which are besetting him and his Christian colleagues (i.e. the persecution which is being waged by the Roman emperor and his pagan servants). The point of this is that even though the Christians may feel that God has abandoned them and allowed them to be taken over by evil forces, God is still in control of the world, and he will have the last word, which will be favorable for the Church.

After the opening scenes and the unleashing of the woes which

God has decreed, there are intermediate visions (7:1-17), which show that the desolation and woe are not total; some are to be spared, so that when God does eventually intervene and decree the final tribulation, only the ones who are hostile to God and his people will suffer at the end. The faithful ones, who have endured the trials patiently in faith, hope and love, will enjoy God's final victory by being admitted to his presence for eternity.

If we read and re-read the text several times, the mist of imagery and symbolism gives way to the underlying pattern, and the essence of the message emerges. It is a consoling assurance that God is in charge of everything; he is even the one who allows his Christian people to suffer trials and persecution, including martyrdom. But evil can never win, because God plans to reward his faithful servants with his own presence.

There is certainly a difference between this book and the earlier Johannine writings which we have already seen. The apocalyptic form is different, and the future-looking promise of the seer differs from the "eternal life here and now" message which comes through in the other works. We can see why people say that a different writer must have produced this book. Nevertheless, we should also notice the underlying sameness in the message, since this is the basic teaching which we attribute ultimately to the Apostle himself. The central figure is still the glorious, divine, all-powerful and all-knowing Jesus. The ultimate promise is still that those who relate to him by faith will share his eternal life in the Father's presence, and that they are already assured of just that because they are persevering against outside pressures which are designed to pull them away from this faith.

As we saw in regard to the earlier Johannine writings, the probability, and even the actual reality, of martyrdom is not at all to be ignored or brushed away. Jesus is ready to expect this much of his friends. But this "first death" will bring them to escape the "second death," which is the loss of heavenly reward after earthly unbelief, and the tragedy of the eternal loss of God's presence.

Once we penetrate the medium and get to the message, we are amazed at how ingeniously these followers of the Beloved Disciple have preserved and interpreted his teaching, and the teaching of Jesus as well. The real variety is on the level of the form: epistle, Gospel, and now apocalypse, which the seer draws from the Old Testament, and adapts to the reality of his contemporary Christian situation.

The Opening Scene (chs. 4-5)

As he did before, in the septet of the letters, the seer again addresses himself to the imagination of those who are to hear his message read to them. We would never get even the minimum of the message if we would try to analyse the details or look at the scene only in a logical way. The word-pictures which the seer presents make impressions, but they do not convey orderly intellectual concepts. This is the language of imagination and fantasy drawn from what we have called the "pre-apocalyptic" visions of the Old Testament seers (especially Ezekiel chs. 1-10). The seer finds himself called by a "trumpet-like voice" (4:1), which suggests overpowering authority, and then he finds himself in an ecstasy (4:2), which means that he is carried beyond his usual conscious state and allowed by God to have a vision of heaven. There he sees God enthroned in divine majesty and royal splendor, surrounded by twenty-four elders who adore and praise him ceaselessly. These elders, it seems, represent the twelve tribes of Israel, doubled now to include also the New Israel, which is the Christian Church.

The four living creatures (4:6 ff.) are puzzling because we find it difficult to picture them in detail. Perhaps it is better if we do not try too hard to do that, and merely see them in our imagination as superhuman creatures who form part of God's heavenly court. The four figures of the lion, the ox, the man and the eagle, appear often in Christian art as symbols of the four evangelists (John is represented by the eagle, because his Gospel "soars" to the heavenly heights more than the Synoptics, who are more down to earth).

The members of the heavenly court praise God and adore him as the only Lord who governs all creation, and who deserves the homage of every creature. Already this is a variation of the old Persian religious symbolism, which spoke of two supreme forces, good and evil, struggling in perpetual conflict, with neither side ever winning.

But the Old Testament seers of Israel adapted that imagery to speak of Jahweh as the only supreme Lord, who tolerates evil but who is always in supreme control of all his creation. Now the Christian seer adapts this style of language again, as he identifies Jesus with God, as the writer of the First Epistle of John and of the Gospel According to John did.

The vision advances to show the scroll, which was the usual form of a book in the ancient world of the seer's day, and which represents here God's decree for all of his creation (the image is in Ezekiel's inaugural vision in Ezk 3, and also in Daniel's apocalyptic vision in Dn 7). The only one who is qualified to open the seven seals is the Lion of Judah and the Offspring of David, who is also the Lamb, once slain but now alive. Obviously, this means that the Risen Lord Jesus is the only one who is qualified to interpret and mediate the plan and decree of God, which is represented here by the scroll. Incidentally, the image of the Lamb is another feature which the Book of Revelation has in common with the Fourth Gospel (Jn 1:29, 36). The Johannine writings are the only ones in the New Testament which speak of Jesus specifically as the Lamb.

Once the Lamb comes upon the scene, the whole picture becomes even more splendid that it was before. The song fragments suggest a victorious and triumphant scene, with the Lamb now ready to take the scroll and break the seven seals, putting into effect thereby the full totality of God's decree.

The First Six Seals (ch. 6)

After the glory and majesty of the long opening scene, the seals themselves are fearful, even repellent. The seer borrows imagery now from Zechariah, who describes God's plan in terms of strange cosmic scenes and bizarre visions (Zc 1-6). The first four visions show that God allows trials to come to the earth. The four horsemen of the Apocalypse imitate the four horsemen of Zc 1, but here they bring war, death, famine and destruction. Under the veil of imagery here the message is that the troubles which the Christian people must endure are not a sign that Satan has conquered God, but rather they are trials which God allows in order to test their faith and to purify them. At the fifth seal the Christian martyrs appear, waiting for God to judge them and give them their reward. But they must wait (6:7); there are to be more martyrs. This, of course, is a major part of the seer's message to his fellow Christians: the Church must be ready to suffer even more before God brings them to their reward.

The sixth seal brings the Day of the Lord. The prophets of the Old Testament, such as Amos (Am 5:18); Isaiah (Is 2:10-21); and Joel (Jl ch. 2), used this phrase to speak of the future time in which God will come and establish his supreme lordship by banishing the unjust and bringing his faithful servants to a final age of endless peace. In the Synoptic Gospels Jesus applied this image to describe his own future return (Mk 8:38; 9:1; ch. 13 etc.). Paul also spoke of "the Day," which now in the Christian setting came to mean the future coming of the Risen Jesus as judge at the end of the world. Now the seer uses the same image to describe the dawning of this great and terrible day. However, for God's faithful and long-suffering Christian servants, both the martyrs who have already died, and for the suffering ones who must still witness, the Day of the Lord will be hopeful, because it will bring them their judgment and the final reward, which will consist of enjoying God's heavenly presence forever. The terror of the sixth seal is fearful only for those who earn God's wrath by their failure to do his will—and in this context, this refers to the Roman pagans who persecute the Christian people.

The Intermediate Visions (ch. 7)

7:1-8   Before the final seal comes, there are two intermediate visions, which come as a relief after the bleakness of the first six seals. The imagery of the Old Testament comes again. The marking off of those who are to be spared in the coming disaster, is an image that we see for the first time in the Book of Exodus (ch. 12), as the blood of the Paschal Lamb smeared on their doorposts marks out the Hebrews for life, while the Egyptians lose their firstborn in death. In Ezekiel 9:4, we see the scene of God sparing those who have a mark on their foreheads (his faithful servants) while all others are to be punished for their idolatry. The twelve tribes of Israel here represent the people of God, amplified now by the symbolic numbers to represent the entire Christian Church (the 144,000), grown to be the completion and perfection of what Israel had originally been. All of these, i.e. the Church of God's people still living and suffering on earth, are to be spared the punishment which the Day of the Lord will bring crashing down on their oppressors, as it struck the Pharaoh and his hostile people in the ancient Exodus event.

7:9-17   The second intermediate vision shows the martyrs who have already died by shedding their blood as Jesus the Lamb shed his on the first Good Friday. They have come through the great trials as Jesus came through his, and they are in his presence, sharing his resurrection-glory and his victory over evil. For them there is only a future of unlimited joy and peace, which the seer describes by the images of 7:15-17. These images, of course, are all merely temporal, since the Old Testament prophets and seers, who originally used them, knew only of temporal happiness, even in the final future age. But in the Christian context, these images are ultimately inadequate, because, in the light of Jesus' saving death and resurrection, and in the light of the heavenly eternity which the Johannine teaching describes, the Church now expects a future which goes beyond the confines of time and space—beyond death itself! However, there are no images which can do justice to such a future, because it is a divine reality which surpasses human imagination and experience.

The Seventh Seal (8:1)

We would expect that the seventh seal would be some kind of finale, but we are surprised to see that it is only a pause, and silence, which represents respect for the majestic presence of God. We might be inclined to suspect at first that originally there was another scene here, which became lost when the second septet was joined to the first one. But the better explanation is that the seer wants to show that the final ending of God's plan (which would be indicated by the seventh seal) is still in the future, and that the decrees of the next septet must be worked through first.

D. The Septet of the Trumpets (8:2-11:19)

We have now another vision in which the seer describes again his view of God's heavenly court with the attending angelic spirits. There are seven scenes again, indicated this time by seven trumpets, since the blowing of a trumpet introduces the announcement of a decree which has been enacted by the supreme ruler. In 10:1-11:14, there are again two intermediate visions, and then comes the seventh trumpet (11:15-19), which introduces the final stage of things, as God has decreed that they are to be.

There is a connection between this septet and the preceding one, so that the two sets of scenes are not merely parallel, but closely intertwined. The 144,000 faithful servants of God who appeared in 7:1-8, reappear there too (8:4; 9:4). But they have been signed with the seal of the living God (7:2-3), and therefore they are to be protected, while the final calamities which God has decided to send, are announced by the trumpets, and then sent from heaven to earth, but only upon the hostile pagans who have earned God's wrath by their idolatry and their hostility to his Church.

8:2-5   The seer watches while the administering angels prepare the seven trumpets. But the incense, which symbolizes adoration, and the prayers of God's people, go up to him, while coals (symbolizing God's wrath) are poured down to earth upon those who are hostile to God and his people.

8:6-9:21   In the description of the woes which the trumpets announce, the seer has combined terminology drawn partly from the Exodus tradition of the plagues which God sent upon the Egyptians, and partly from the "pre-apocalyptic" imagery of the prophet Joel. The result, as we see in the first four woes, is a picture of dreadful disasters, so that life become simply unbearable, for those who have these woes come upon them, i.e. for everyone except the holy servants of God who have been set apart by God's protection, and thus are spared these final woes.

The fifth and sixth trumpets announce woes which come in slightly longer scenes, but basically the point is the same as in the preceding woes. The image of destroying locusts draws partly from the plagues of Egypt (Ps 78:46; 105:34), and partly from the vivid oracle of Joel (Jl 1). This woe (announced by the fifth trumpet) comes upon the Roman empire from out of the abyss (9:1-2), i.e. from the regions of hell below the earth, whereas the first four woes descended from heaven above. This means that God can send his wrath in any form that he chooses, since all creation, below as well as above, is subject to his decree. However, it is not to come upon his faithful servants (9:3), but only upon their persecutors.

There is a special quality to the sixth trumpet, because of the geographical detail of the Euphrates river (9:14), and the military flavor which characterizes the invaders in this scene. One respectable explanation is that the seer is describing the Parthians, who were threatening in his day to invade the eastern area of the Roman empire. This means that God is allowing this prospect of military disaster to shake the failing strength of the pagan empire, in punishment for its hostility to God and for its failure to serve him. But, as the seer says in the closing verses of the scene (9:20-21), these pagans fail to learn the lesson, and they continue their idolatry and their estrangement from God and from his law and word.

The Intermediate Visions (10:1-11:14)

The great burden of woe and calamity is now about to give way to a more hopeful vision of the final glory which is to come to God's faithful servants, i.e. to the 144,000 who have been signed with the seal of the living God (7:2-3; 9:4). These two scenes which the seer now reports, allow a breathing space, or a moment of consolation, to his Christian colleagues who are hearing his prophetic report, and prepare them for the promise which comes with the seventh trumpet (11:15-19).

10:1-11   Both of these intermediate visions are more obscure and puzzling than the corresponding ones in the preceding septet. Nevertheless, we can make out the basic content, and see that the mighty angel (10:1) has a special message for the seer now. The vision of the scroll adapts the imagery of Ezekiel's inaugural vision (Ez 3:1) again, to tell the seer and his friends that there is more to come (10:5-7), and that beyond all the woes which the seals and the trumpets have shown, there is still one more trumpet to go. Only after this final decree will God's plan be completed. And since there has been so much calamity, there is reason to hope that the seventh trumpet will announce something good. Sweet and sour are combined in the scroll as the seer eats it, as Ezekiel did in his vision, since God has decreed that there is still to be a mixture of pain and peace.

11:1-14   Zechariah (ch. 2) presents the image of the man measuring off the area which is to be spared, while whatever is outside it will be subject to the great coming devastation which God is about to send. In the jumbled text of his fourth chapter, the same prophet speaks of his vision of the two olive trees and the two lampstands, which represent God's two appointed representatives (whoever they may be).

All of this is in the Old Testament background now, as the seer adapts these images to his Chrisitan situation. The Church is to be the new protected area, but the pagans will be allowed to trouble them temporarily (for the forty-two months). Just as Moses and Elijah (11:3, 6 ff.) witnessed to the true God before the pagan kings in the Old Testament time, now the Christians will carry on the work of these prophets for the New Testament time. But they will be persecuted, ridiculed and martyred as their predecessors were. Nevertheless, in the end, after the time of trial (represented by the forty-two months, or the three and one-half days, or whatever the symbolic numbers may mean), the martyrs will be admitted to God's presence (11:12), and the city of their oppressors (the "Sodom" or "Egypt" which represents the Old Testament receivers of God's punishing wrath, and which is now pagan Rome), will be crushed, and by the terror of this experience, many will be converted to the true God (11:13).

Seventh Trumpet: Finale (11:15-19)

Now that the trials are past, and the Church's persecutors have had to endure the woes of the six trumpets, the seventh angel blows the final trumpet. The seer presents the final scene as the ultimate victory celebration of the members of God's heavenly court. There, in the final stage of God's plan, there are no more enemies or persecutors; there is only the triumphant song of God's adorers, the twenty-four elders who symbolize ancient Israel and their counterparts in the Christian Church. Jesus is with the Lord as "his Anointed One" (which means "his Christ" in 11:15). These adoring elders appeared at the beginning of the former septet (4:9-11) with their song of praise to God, and now they conclude the second septet with another song of praise (11:17-18). It may well be that these song fragments, like so many scattered throughout Revelation, are from the early liturgy, as the Ephesian Christians celebrated it in the first century, praising God for his promises, which gave them hope in spite of their trials.

In the last verse of the septet (11:19) the seer can see heaven, and in it he sees the temple, the ark of the covenant, and a display of cosmic storms. All three of these elements are from the rich collection of Old Testament images which symbolize God's presence among his people. So the last scene of this vision shows the seer a reassurance that God is "all in all." To the troubled Christians who are to receive this message, and who should recognize the imagery because of their familiarity with the Old Testament, the entire succession of scenes in both the septets adds up to a message of hope: their troubles are permitted by God to give them an opportunity to show their faith in him under persecution. This assimilates them to Jesus, and those who persevere as Jesus did, and as the faithful Old Testament witnesses did in their day, will be admitted to the heavenly court and to eternal joy. This should encourage his friends, the seer hopes, to endure even martyrdom if it should become necessary. The fourth evangelist has tried to urge them along the same path, as we have seen.

Questions for Consideration and Reflection

1. Why does the seer place so much emphasis on the number seven in these chapters?
2. What was the situation in the seer's own time and place that formed the background of his message to his fellow Christians?
3. How is the second septet (the trumpets) related to the first one (the seals)?
4. How does the seer adapt the future promise of the Old Testament images which he uses, to the new Christian reality?
5. Who are the twenty-four elders? Who are the 144,000 who are sealed?
6. Why is there no final scene for the seventh seal?

13

MORE VISIONS AND ANOTHER SEPTET

"The huge dragon, the ancient serpent known as the devil or Satan, the seducer of the whole world, was driven out; he was hurled down to earth and his minions with him" (Rv 12:9).

Preliminary Reading

Read Rv 12-16, writing down your observations and your comments as you read. Notice especially the following details:
1. The Old Testament images which the seer adapts;
2. The song fragments (12:10-12; 15:3-4; 16:5-7);
3. The seer's veiled references to persons and events contemporary to himself;
4. The theological message which comes across in the form of the apocalyptic imagery.

The seer has a remarkable way of building the sections of his apocalypse into one another, so that one passage seems to lead directly into the next. We saw this when the septet of the trumpets grew naturally out of the septet of the seals. Now, from the final scene of the seventh trumpet, with its picture of heaven and the overpowering presence of God in the images of the temple, the ark of the covenant and the storm (11:19), there is an easy transition to a whole new set of scenes. There also happen to be seven of them here (chs. 12-14), but they do not constitute a septet as the other scenes did; rather, they are individual pictures, with a total impact that even seems somewhat repetitious. Then comes the third septet (the bowls, or the plagues) in chapters 15-16. This septet also differs from the preceding septets in its pattern, since it does not have the intermediate visions with their momentary relief before the final scene. Nevertheless, we find ourselves a bit accustomed by now to the bizarre style of the seer's language, and we may find that the essence of his theological message is beginning to appear more clearly than it did earlier. This is a good sign, of course, since it means that we are penetrating the veil of the seer's literary form, and grasping the deeper level of his message.

A. The Visions (chs. 12-14)

The seer certainly has the language and the images of the Old Testament at his fingertips, since he can draw elements from it so readily. Yet, he is able to transpose these images so that they show an essential continuity between their original biblical meaning, and the new Christian situation to which he applies them. In this collection of seven visions between the second and third septets, we get the impression of all the collected power of satanic evil thrown full-force against the Church, but without being able to destroy it. Instead of being defeated, the Church produces more martyrs, who then enjoy a share in the resurrection-glory of Jesus—all of which must have been a welcome, if demanding, reassurance to the Johannine Christians of Domitian's empire in the seer's day.

The Dragon, the Woman and Michael (chapter 12)

There appear to be two visions here that may have been independent of each other originally, before they were combined in the present form of the chapter. In any case, we can recognize readily the familiar image of the woman, which the Old Testament prophets used repeatedly to depict Israel, the beloved people whom God had espoused to himself in covenant love. We can also see a puzzling interplay of features in the evil monster who is now a dragon (12:3 etc.) and now a serpent (12:9, 15). The fearful picture of this monster draws together the ancient image of the primordial serpent which the Jahwist editor depicted in Gn 3, and the hostile beast of Dn 7:7, which symbolizes the oppressors of God's people.

We have seen representations of Mary as the Woman of the Apocalypse, standing on the moon and crowned with twelve stars, holding the child Jesus in her arms. These depictions, in statues or in pictures, show how readily Christian artists recognize possible references to God's mother in the Scripture. But we need to recognize also the conscious intention of the seer here, and it is more likely that he wanted to show a combination of figures. On the one hand he depicts in this scene of the Old Testament people of Israel, represented by the prophetic image of the woman loved by God (e.g. Is 62:5), and by her crown, which suggests Israel's ancient federation of the twelve tribes. She produces the child, Jesus, destined to rule the nations with his royal scepter (12:5), which repeats the royal image of Ps 2:9. The child (Jesus), who is thus the messianic ruler born from God's beloved people of the Old Testament, is now taken to heaven ("lifted up," as the fourth evangelist says of Jesus' resurrection-glory, e.g., Jn 3:14 etc.). This frustrates the monster (Satan), but he is to have even more frustration. The woman, who is now the Church, essentially continuous and identical with the original Old Testament people of God, escapes him too, by being taken to the desert (12:6), which was the Old Testament place of Israel's honeymoon with God, where he showered her with signs of his providence and powerful protection. The 1260 days are equivalent to the forty-two months, or the three and one-half years, which the seer adapts from the scenes of

Dn 7:25 and 12:7, to suggest the full duration of Israel's time of enduring enemy persecution, before God intervenes, defeats the oppressor and inaugurates the final age of peace.

12:7-12   The scene of Michael warring with the dragon seems to break in, since the woman and her child return in 12:13-17. In any case, Michael's defeat of the dragon (which is now also the serpent) transfers here to the Christian situation the original apocalyptic scene of Daniel 10-12. Now, instead of Old Testament Israel protected by the heavenly angel against the Greeks, it is the Christian Church protected by God against the pagan power of the Roman empire. Incidentally, there is another New Testament scene—in v. 9 of the Epistle of Jude—in which the same Michael battles with the devil. It seems that this image circulated in the late Old Testament period, and was known also among the Jewish Christians who had the Book of Daniel in their religious heritage, as well as the new faith which could transfer this imagery to the context of the Church.

Not all Bibles print the victory song (12:10-12) in verse form, although the *New American Bible* does. But, like the song fragment in the preceding chapter (11:17-18), this one celebrates the loyalty of the martyrs (12:11), and promises heaven to the Christians who now find themselves facing the prospect of the supreme test of their faith. Maybe these are parts of hymns which the Johannine Christians sang in the early Ephesian prayer meetings!

12:13-17   The previous scene returns briefly, but this time the woman appears along with the image of the eagle's wings, which symbolize God's power and protection in the Sinai scene of Ex 19:4, and in the Song of Moses (Dt 32:11). The Church is under God's protection against Satan, just as Israel was under his care during the desert experience of the ancient Exodus! But the serpent is not about to give up: he spews a flood of water to wash away the woman (this symbolizes the Roman empire, sent by Satan to engulf and destroy the Church). It does not work. But, as before, the war is not over yet; Satan's servant (the empire) will continue, for awhile, to attack faithful Christian witnesses.

Beasts From Sea and Land (chapter 13)

13:1-10   One evil produces another. Now the dragon of chapter 12 (Satan) passes on its power to a new monster, a fearful beast from the sea, with many heads and many horns. The seer draws this figure also from the apocalyptic Book of Daniel but here it means not four enemy peoples against Israel, as it does in Dn 7, but the one combined hostility of the Roman empire, with its sensuality, its idolatry and its emperor-cult. From the seer's perspective, in Ephesus, or anywhere in that area, the sea can readily represent the West, and suggest that the attack comes from the direction of Italy, moving towards the Christians of the Johannine Church!

The Roman empire, sponsored by Satan, receives homage and allegiance from peoples who are too small and weak to resist (13:4). But here again the seer is·the supreme realist. He combines the image of the Lamb's book of life, meaning the list of those who will enjoy his presence after the trial, with the call for endurance in 13:10. Some must still face captivity and the sword; the Johannine Church must not deceive itself by false hopes; only those who persevere all the way, to martyrdom if need be, can expect to see the final reward.

13:11-18   After the dragon/serpent and the beast from the sea, the next beast, coming from the land, is a bit more problematic. He seems able to do wondrous things, such as bringing fire from heaven to earth. This suggests that this beast is some kind of false prophet who imitates the legitimate prophets of God, and seduces faithful Christians by getting them to follow the lead of the pagans. Jesus warned his friends against false prophets in his parting words (Mt 24:24), before his Passion, so the seer seems to know what he is doing when he presents this scene!

Some of these features are ugly caricatures, which mock Jesus and his faithful servants. The sea beast is wounded but alive (13:3); the land beast can work miracles (13:13-14); and the followers of the beast are marked with its name (13:16-17), as a counterforce to the 144,000 faithful Christians who are signed with the seal of God in 7:1-8. Whatever may have been the precise original meaning of these details, the overall effect comes through, as the number-name of the beast emerges in 13:18, to tantalize the curiosity of those who receive the seer's message. Commentators down the ages have offered ingenious interpretations of the beast's number-name, often identifying him with enemies of the Church during the various centuries of the Christian era. This depended, of course, on the basic assumption that the text was a prediction of the future. But, if we take it as the seer's veiled description of the divine and human realities which he saw operating in his own day, then we can see the 666 as a device resulting from the number value of some Greek letters (since te seer wrote in Greek), which spell the name of "Nero-Caesar." However, since Nero died in 68 A.D., the seer may mean it as a veiled reference to Domitian, who was emperor from 81 to 96, and whose hostility to Christians made his reign seem like a renewal of the Nero time.

The Lamb and His Companions (14:1-5)

It would be difficult not to appreciate the peaceful scene of the Lamb and his friends, after the fearful scenes of the dragon/serpent and the beasts. It repeats images which we have seen in the first septet, and shows that now everyone is under the total control of the beast. Mount Zion of 14:1 is, as we know, the site of Jerusalem even today. But here it seems to be rather the new Zion which the Old Testament prophets describe as the restored place of final peace for God's people, after their trials have passed and they are finally purified (Mi 4:6; Jl 3:5; Zp 3:12-20). This earthly image now refers to the heavenly Zion however, since Christians now look ahead to the final peace which surpasses the limits of any earthly city, beyond all time and space. The 144,000 faithful servants reappear, singing their victory song, which only they may sing, since they have remained chaste. This is another Old Testament image, which reverses the original image of harlotry or adultery as a sin of the heart, meaning that some Israelites deserted Jahweh and followed the pagan cults, instead of remaining faithful to the covenant obligations which they had inherited from Moses (Am 5:2; Is 1:21). Those who have remained chaste, therefore, are now those who have maintained their fidelity to Jesus, in the face of pagan pressure.

Three Angels and Four Voices (14:6-13)

The shift toward the final peace which began with the vision of the Lamb and his companions, now becomes more definite. The impression comes through that the seer is beginning to pull his message to a new level. The atmosphere of ultimate victory is in the air now, in spite of the repulsive monsters which made their appearance in the previous scenes, and in spite of the fact that the time of trial is not yet in the past.

14:6-7;8   The first two angels come and go briefly, but their message is both demanding and reassuring. The first one announces that at last God is about to sit in judgment. This is what the martyrs wanted back in the first septet (6:10), but they had to be patient, because it was not yet time for their vindication. We are soon to see the final unfolding of God's plan, which was announced by the angel with the scroll (10:7), before the seventh trumpet sounded!

The second angel announces that the great city of Babylon has finally fallen, after forcing many peoples to share her lewdness. Again here the seer transposes to his Christian context the Old Testament image of the empire which had persecuted and enslaved God's Israelite people, as well as the sexual image which the prophets use to represent the pagan cults. Now the announcement prepares for the seer's longer dirge over fallen Rome, which will come in chapter 18.

14:9-13   The third angel's announcement also declares doom and reckoning for the pagan oppressors who serve the beast rather than God. The image of a cup of God's wrath looks partly back to the prophetic use of this figure in the Old Testament (e.g. Is 51:17; Jr 25:15 ff.), and partly ahead to the bowls, which will release divine punishment on the Church's attackers in the third septet (chs. 15-16).

14:13   Time after time the seer presents the frightening but consoling truth: death is not improbable. There have been martyrs (6:9-11); and there will be more (13:9-10). Now he says it again, but this time he makes the point in the form of a promise of the happiness that they will find, as the record of their faith and endurance will merit for them the reward of enjoying God's presence, and that of the Lamb.

In all of this it seems that the seer is not distinguishing clearly between heaven and earth, and that for this reason the perspective is somewhat blurred. But it may be because we forget what he is doing. He is reporting to his friends the things that he has seen under the influence of an ecstasy, as he said at the beginning of his message (1:10). For him, earth and heaven are joined because they are both equally under God's dominion, and, ultimately, what the seer has come to know by his prophetic intuition, is God's view of all things and his plan for history. And from this perspective, the short-term pains which now burden the troubled Christians, are well worth enduring, for the sake of the endless peace which will be their final reward. This message is somewhat similar to the promise that Jesus left with his disciples at the Last Supper, as the fourth evangelist preserves it in Jn 15:18-27; 16:20-22. Of course, the Gospel form is vastly different from the apocalyptic form, but as we come to see more and more, the message of the Beloved Disciple comes through both, as a call to a demanding faith, and to the prospect of accepting martyrdom, if it comes to it, as well as the promise of eternal life (Jn 14:18-21; 16:33).

The Great Harvest (14:14-20)

The Third Isaiah delivered an oracle early in the post-exilic era (about 500 B.C.), about the grapes and the wine press, as an image of vengeance against enemies (Is 63:1-6). About two centuries after that, Joel gave his contemporaries another prophetic oracle (Jl 4:13-16), which combines the images of the grain being harvested and the newly-picked grapes being crushed in the press. Both these oracles use agricultural images to suggest reckoning and judgment, as the master comes to collect the just return which is due to him.

The seer finds these oracles helpful because of the theme of just judgment and reckoning, which he can now apply to Jesus' negative judgment of the Roman empire and its treatment of his followers. We might wonder about the identity of the Son of Man who wields the harvesting sickle (14:14). The figure recalls the apocalyptic vision of Daniel (ch. 7), which Jesus often applied to himself, although originally in the setting of the Old Testament, the image represents puny and oppressed Israel, which is eventually raised up by God as judge of the former attackers. So the seer could be using the image here to mean Jesus, or the Church. However, since the Son of Man here is wearing a crown (14:14), the seer probably wants to suggest Jesus himself, whom he always depicts in Revelation as glorious, supreme and victorious.

Nevertheless, we may feel some hesitation at seeing Jesus in the image of a destroying judge. It is a long way from the lamb—meek before the shearer! Still, all we can do is accept what the biblical writers give us. True enough, the earlier images of Jesus stress his meekness and kindness, as the bringer of God's healing favor (Lk 4:18-19). But Jesus spoke of himself several times as the Son of Man (e.g. Mk 8:31; 9:31; 10:33-34); so it is understandable that eventually the apostolic preachers spoke of him as the one raised up by God— like the Son of Man of Daniel 7—and who was to return as judge (Ac 17:31), and even as destroyer (2 Th 2:8).

We must admit that the Johannine teaching is not very kind or gentle toward enemies. The apostates of 1 John are "anti-Christs" whom the brethren must avoid. "The Jews" and "the world" in the Fourth Gospel are consistently hostile to Jesus, and the fourth evangelist makes no attempt to cover up his hostility to them. So now, in the light of all this, it should not surprise us that the seer has absorbed the Johannine dislike of enemies, especially of the Roman pagans. It simply shows us that Jesus' teaching about loving enemies (Mt 5:44) had a long way to go before his followers would absorb it. Even today we still have to acknowledge that Christians have not mastered this, even among themselves, much less toward enemies!

B. The Septet of the Bowls (chs. 15-16)

In the third and last of the septets (the bowls) we come upon what has been a familiar pattern. The flavor of the Old Testament is here, since the seer obviously has borrowed terminology from his favorite source, and adapted it to his own situation.

15:1-4   One of the most stirring songs in the Old Testament is the Red Sea Song of Ex 15, which has also been called the Song of Moses or the Song of Miriam. It comes immediately after the narrative of the Israelites' crossing of the Red Sea, as God protects them from their Egyptian pursuers and the hostile Pharaoh. Now the Johannine seer ingeniously applies this basic pattern to the picture of the martyrs, who have come through the period of testing and are now victorious in God's heavenly presence.

The seer also reintroduces here several elements which have occurred in earlier scenes of Revelation: the sea of glass from the first septet (4:6); the Lamb's companions with their harps, from the previous chapter (14:1-5); the beast, with its image and its number-name from the scene of 13:11-18, and, of course, the Lamb again, with the new Song of Moses. We wonder whether the seer was thinking here of the Paschal Lamb, which figured prominently in the Jewish ritual of Passover, along with Moses and the Exodus victory which the Song celebrated (Ex 15). In any case, now he speaks of the one song which is that of both Moses and the Lamb. Yet, the fact that the ones who sing this song are the ones who have conquered the beast and are now victorious, along with the fact that they are now in heaven, suggests that they are the martyrs, whose trial is over now, and who can rejoice and glorify God, as they do in the song (15:3-4).

15:5-8   The preliminary vision of God's heavenly court with his victorious Christian martyrs, gives way now to that of the four attending creatures, and the seven angels with the seven bowls of God's wrath. The smoke which fills the scene and suggests God's invisible glory, recalls the cloud of God's presence, which appeared in the desert over the portable shrine (Ex 40:35), and also the majesty of God's heavenly court which Isaiah saw in his inaugural vision (Is 6:4). The seer contrasts this with the plagues which are to descend from heaven and strike God's earthly enemies.

Ch. 16   Again, in the plagues, we can see the influence which the Old Testament traditions have had on the seer. This time it is the tradition of the ten plagues of Egypt, which we find in Ex 7-12; (also Ps 78; 105; Ws 11-19). As he adapts the original themes to the new

Christian context, the seer inserts another song fragment (16:5-7), which shows again the same vindictive attitude towards persecutors as the one which we saw in the scene of the Great Harvest (13:14-20). When we look even more closely at this fragment, however, we notice that it is no more specifically Christian than the one which we saw in the previous chapter (15:3-4), and we wonder whether they may have both come from the seer's Jewish background, and been adapted to this Christian apocalyptic message. This does not justify the violence of such hatred of enemies, of course, but it helps us to see that only gradually did the Church evolve away from its Jewish roots, preserving familiar elements of its Old Testament heritage, even though they were counter to the universal love which Jesus taught.

The sixth plague has a geographical reference to the East and to "the great river Euphrates," like the sixth trumpet (9:12-21). Likewise, the seer brings back the images of Satan, the emperor and the false prophet, and seems to be alluding to a catastrophic war, which will test the power of the Romans. "The great day of God almighty" draws from the prophetic theme of the Day of the Lord, which will be God's final display of his justice and power, and "Armageddon," which even has passed into our English vocabulary as a synonym for a definitive conflict. It recalls Megiddo, and rightly so, since this area of Northern Palestine (Galilee) was the site of battles from the early years of the Old Testament period (Jg 5:19; 2Ch 35:20-24). Now the seer transfers the term to apply to the definitive encounter of God with the forces of the pagan empire.

The outcome of this final battle comes in the seventh bowl, which unleashes the seventh plague on the earth. But this great devastation is to harm only the pagans who are left, since all of God's faithful servants have been taken to heaven (15:2-4). This is why there is no escape for anyone who is on the earth when the seventh plague comes. "Babylon," which the seer has used before to symbolize Rome, must drink the cup of wrath; this image has occurred before too (14:10), as the seer drew it from the prophetic preaching of the Second Isaiah (Is 51:17), as well as from that of Jeremiah (Jr 25:15-17) and Ezekiel (Ez 23:31-34). The whole scene of the final plague looks like the end of the world, with only doom for the pagans. There are not even any last minute conversions this time, as there were in the septet of the trumpets (11:13); it is too late even for that now. This is why the voice of God says, "It is finished!" (16:17). God is bringing on the final stage of his decree.

Questions for Consideration and Reflection

1. How does the seer adapt the Old Testament themes of the Day of the Lord, and of the Exodus tradition, to his Christian situation?

2. How does the seer relate the dragon/serpent, the beasts and the Lamb? What is the origin of these figures in the Old Testament?

3. Do the visions of these chapters advance the theological message beyond that of the preceding chapters?

4. Is there any significant difference between the theological emphasis of Revelation and that of 1 John and the Gospel According to John?

5. What does the seer mean by the images of the woman (ch. 12), Mount Zion (14:1), the Great Harvest (14:14-20), Babylon (14:8), and Armageddon (16:6)?

6. Does the seer deliberately set out to offer a prophetic message to the Christian people of our time?

14

THE PROMISE OF PEACE

"He will wipe away all tears from their eyes;
there will be no more death,
and no more mourning or sadness.
The world of the past is gone" (Rv 21:4).

Preliminary Reading

Read Rv 17-22. Write down your observations and comments as you read along. Try to notice especially these features of the section:
1. The seer's optimism for the future;
2. The images which the seer repeats here from earlier sections of Revelation;
3. The violence in the destruction of the enemies;
4. The variety of the images of Jesus.

There has been a shift in the atmosphere of the seer's message. After the septets and the intervening visions, with so many woes and trials for both the faithful Christians and their pagan oppressors, the view now moves toward the final stage of God's decree for history. There is a good bit of repetition in the basic message of these final chapters, as well as in some of the images, which we have already seen in the earlier scenes of the book. Perhaps these final scenes, or at least some of them, were originally separate, before the seer combined them in the present form, to make one final book. This could explain what seems like duplication of themes and scenes within this section; it may explain also why these chapters repeat some elements of the message which the seer has presented already in the earlier parts of Revelation.

In any case, there is something new here. The faithful Christians have been signed with God's seal, so they are now under his protection. All that remains now is for the seer to show the final destruction of their enemies, and the final reward which God has in store for his Church. All the oppressive things are to move into the background now, and the closing chapters are a collage of images which the seer draws mostly from the Old Testament (as usual), to show the heavenly city, which is the Church, finally blessed with peace.

A. The Destruction of "Babylon" (17:1-19:4)

We noticed before that the seer builds one section of his message into another. He does it here too, linking this chapter to the preceding septet by showing one of the seven angels, who introduces him to a new vision. This same angel will appear again to introduce him to the heavenly Jerusalem in 21:9. It is a relief, of course, to see an angel from the septet of the bowls doing anything pleasant, since the bowls are full of plagues which God sends to earth—but only onto the ones who oppress his faithful servants!

17:1-18 This angel brings the seer to see two women, one evil and the other good. The evil one named "Babylon," is the very quintessence of harlotry, which is a favorite Old Testament symbol of paganism, and of a heart not in true union with God. The cup of lewdness which the harlot holds is also an Old Testament image, adapted from the oracle of Jeremiah (Jr 51:7), to symbolize a whole lifestyle of evil and perversion, totally incompatible with Christianity and even hostile to it, since the woman is now drunk with the blood of Christian martyrs (17:6). The scarlet beast, with its seven heads and ten horns, has already appeared in the vision of 13:1-10, as the symbol of the empire. Once the angel explains (17:9) that the beast's seven heads represent the seven hills, we can immediately recognize the mysterious allusion to the geography of the city of Rome. The explanation about the emperors and the subject kings, is confusing (17:10 ff.), but the thrust of the angel's message seems to be that Rome, city and empire, along with its emperors, past, present and future, as well as its subject kings, will never prevail over the Lamb and his followers (17:14), who are Jesus and his Church (14:15).

We have seen these images before too, so by now it should not be too difficult to read the whole pattern of this chapter. In the light of the various figures which have recurred often enough by now to be familiar, we see the whole chapter as an introduction to the next vision, which continues the theme of Babylon—Rome's unsuccessful attack against the Lamb.

18:1-24   There are a number of passages in the prophetic literature of the Old Testament which contain satires and maledictions against the pagans. We may wince when we read these chapters now, from a Christian perspective, but the simple truth is that these prophets did not speak from a Chritian perspective, and they had no love for their enemies and oppressors! The oracles of malediction which the seer adapts here are principally from Isaiah (Is 23-24 and 47, against Tyre and Babylon); Jeremiah (Jr 50-51, which are especially long curses of Babylon) and Ezekiel (Ez 26-27, against Tyre). In these prophetic curses we see several phrases and images which serve the seer now, as he adapts them to show his Christian contemporaries a word-picture of Rome burning to the ground in total devastation, with not a single person to pity or rescue. We have already had a brief preview of this kind of oracle in the angelic message of 14:8. But that message was so brief that we may have passed it by without absorbing its impact!

This chapter, however, is so vivid and well-phrased that the effect continues to build up all the way to the end. The overall effect is horrific: God has taken care to rescue all his people first (18:4), and then decreed that the whole city should be destroyed, along with all of its immeasurable wealth and luxury, as well as its lewdness and sensuality (which symbolize Rome's pagan idol-cult and its failure to be converted to the truth of Jesus and his Church).

Nobody comes to the rescue of the doomed city. There is here a touch of cruel irony—there is no honor among thieves, or among evildoers in general! All of those who have consorted with the harlot now keep their distance and do nothing to help the dying city (18:9-10). Likewise the merchants and seamen who grew wealthy from trading with Rome, buying and selling, importing and exporting merchandise, stand back, terrified, as they watch the destruction. But they are afraid also, and do not even lift a finger to help. Once God decides to strike in wrath, no human power can help! This is the cumulative impact of the imagery, up to verse 19.

But the finishing touches come in the last verses of the chapter, and the first few verses of the next one. Another angel sums up the whole of God's decree for his enemy, by adapting the final verses of Jeremiah's oracle (Jr 51) to this situation. The image shifts now from the burnt out harlot-city, to the millstone hurled into the sea. In either image, the effect is the same: Babylon—pagan Rome is finished!

18:20; 19:1-4   The second septet concludes with a victory song (11:15-19), after the bowls of God's wrath have been poured out on the Church's persecutors. Now the same pattern recurs, as all the members of God's heavenly court adore God's majesty (19:4), and sing "Alleluia"—the first time that this Hebrew phrase ("Praise Jahweh!") appears in the New Testament! All the trials of the martyrs and of the Church are past now, and all the powers of evil have been destroyed.

Again, as before, we can wonder about the vindictiveness of this final scene. It simply does not seem Christian. How can even God's victorious saints in heaven gloat over the prospect of divine revenge upon those who did not have the gift of faith?

We would make a mistake of self-deception if we would try to explain away this anomaly too easily. It is real. The real explanation is in the uncompromising dualism of Johannine theology. Throughout the Johannine Literature we have seen a "hard line" attitude towards any and all who do not share the full apostolic faith as the Beloved Disciple has preached it. Whether the offenders be the apostates and "anti-Christs" of 1 John or "the Jews" or "the world" of the Fourth Gospel, or the pagan Roman empire under the lurid imagery of the seer's apocalyptic message, there can be no middle ground. The reason seems to be similar to the firm stand that Paul took on various moral questions when he wrote his First Epistle to the Corinthians (e.g. chs. 5-10). In those days when the Christian faith was young, and other values still exerted powerful alternative influences on shaky members of the primitive Church, the apostolic teachers could not indulge in the luxury of "brinkmanship." It had to be all the way, or nothing. The Church could not expect or hope to draw strength or help from the non-Christian culture that surrounded it. And especially when these non-Christians were hostile pagans, there could be no dealing with them. It meant holding on to the faith and absorbing blows from outside, without being able to hope for an improvement in the situation. This is why John drew his lines in such stark terms, insisting that the only alternative to the full Christian faith in Jesus as eternal God in human form, was separation from the Church, and that meant no eternal life! This put all non-Christians in the same basic category, black, as distinct from white. The prospect of erring in good faith did not appeal to John. For him the only alternative to being a committed Christian ready for martyrdom, was to be a follower of Satan, death and darkness. Theologians are more nuanced nowadays, especially about the consciences and convictions of non-Catholic Christians. But the message of Saint John is not so delicate in this area. He expects martyrdom. That will make his Christian followers like Jesus.

B. The Lamb's Marriage-Feast (19:5-10)

After the heavenly victory-song (19:1-4), the little scene of the Lamb's wedding celebration seems to be a brief appendix to the destruction of the enemies. It is something like the fairy-tale which ends with the "happy-ever-after—following upon the defeat of the evil enemy!" Here, as Jesus is united finally and completely with his Church, the image of the bride reverses the repulsive image of the harlot, and restores the original figure of Israel as God's chosen bride-people, which several Israelite prophets used to speak of the ancient Exodus period, when the desert time represented the honeymoon. Here (19:8) the bride's dress, made of the best white linen, represents the good deeds of the saints, which means principally their endurance and their willing acceptance of martyrdom. This is the most glorious thing that dignifies the Church, and earns for her the love of her spouse, the victorious Lamb who was slain but lives now in resurrection-glory.

We may notice a familiar ring in the angel's words in 19:9. This saying, which is one of the "seven Beatitudes of the Apocalypse" (since they all begin with "Happy are . . ."), is now a part of our eucharistic liturgy. The priest (or other minister) adjusts these words slightly before distributing Holy Communion, and says, "This is the Lamb of God . . . happy are those who are called to his supper." This means that when we share in the sacrament of the eucharist, we are sharing in Jesus' union with his whole faithful Church; it also means that we are receiving a pledge of eternal life, which we will have with him, when our time of trial is past.

C. The Final Contest (19:11-20:15)

19:11-16   This next section brings the seer's last fearful visions, so that after they are out of the way, the only thing that remais will be the happy ending.

We have seen the various images that John has used to describe Jesus in Revelation; he is *the Lamb, the Lion, the Root of David* (5:5-6), as well as the Son of Man (1:13), the Child of the Woman (12:4-5) and the Bridegroom (19:7). But now we are somewhat surprised to see the word-picture of Jesus as a destroying warrior! Nevertheless, after what we have seen of Johannine theology, with its insistence on the total supremacy of Jesus, it may be more understandable for us. The seer's point is that Jesus, who is glorious because he is divine and victorious over evil in his passion and resurrection, symbolized here by his bloodstained cloak (19:3), has all the power of heaven at his command and uses it to overcome the rebellion and hostility of puny humans who do not know enough to accept him as King of Kings and Lord of Lords! Also, just as Jesus is supreme in heavenly glory (ch. 5), likewise he is also supremely powerful over human forces who are still on earth.

The iron scepter of 19:15 shows that Jesus is actually ruling over all humans, as he was destined to do according to the image of his birth as the child of the woman in 12:5. The treading of the winepress in the same verse repeats the image of the Great Harvest from 14:14 ff., showing that this part of God's plan is also about to be carried out, as Jesus exercises judgment and demands the reckoning from those who have oppressed his people.

19:17-21 Another image comes from the prophets to serve the seer's purpose; it is the horrible slaughter-feast of Ezekiel's Gog-Magog oracle (Ezk 39:17-20). This is one of Ezekiel's most repellent sections, in which he pictures Israel's enemies being defeated in battle by God, and their bodies left as carrion for birds of prey. Now the seer adapts this scene to show the fate of the human rebels whom Jesus the warrior has defeated in the preceding scene. We can recognize the images of the two beasts who appeared for the first time in chapter 13 (symbols of the Roman empire and of the false prophet who leads people astray by teaching them to follow the pagan emperor). All of these now have met their match, and there is no escape from Jesus' power, as he wields the sword which comes out of his mouth—as it did in Rv 1:16—the image that shows the power of God's word to decide and control human affairs.

20:1-6 In the scene of the thousand-year chaining of Satan, we see the great conflict come to a close, because the power of God is overcoming the power of evil. Perhaps the first defeat of the dragon represents the resurrection of Jesus, which broke Satan's power to keep men in sin. This opens the entrance of heaven for those who share Jesus' victory by being members of his Church, and for those who have witnessed faithfully to him by being beheaded as martyrs (20:4). They now share "the first resurrection" with Jesus in the fifth Beatitude of the Apocalypse (20:6), and they share the thrones of judgment (20:4), like the twelve Apostles to whom Jesus promised this reward (Mt 19:28), and like the "saints of the Most High" of the apocalyptic scene of Daniel 7:18, which is probably the source of this part of the seer's message.

20:7-10   It seems that John (the seer, that is) has put together two scenes here, to show that even though Satan has been defeated by Jesus' resurrection and by the faithful witness of the Christian martyrs, he will be allowed to try again to molest the Church. The time perspective becomes blurred here, and it is difficult for us to see what comes before or after. But the fact that Satan is released from his prison in the abyss (20:7), suggests that he is to have one last chance. Like Gog and Magog who attack Israel in Ezekiel's "pre-apocalyptic" oracle (Ezk 38-39), Satan, along with the other beasts (the empire and the false prophet), is crushed by fire from heaven and thrown into endless torture.

This is the seer's last description of the Church's enemies. He has made the same point several times, under the form of various images, which may have been combined from several smaller booklets, as we have said. This would explain the many repetitions of the same themes, and even of the same images. But, now that the persecutors are out of the way—and horribly at that—the way is clear for the Last Judgment, and then for the "happy-ever-after" part of the message, the promise of future peace.

20:11-15   God sits on his throne of royal majesty and power, as all the forces of creation are humbled, in his presence (20:11). Even those who have died are now to undergo his judgment. But since the saints have come to share in Jesus' "first resurrection" (20:6), now the "second death" of eternal torture is the only thing that awaits the others, since their names were not on the list of those who were to live because of their faith.

D. The New Heaven and New Earth (21:1-22:5)

This "grand finale" has been worth waiting for! Only God and his people remain, because all the others have been defeated and sent to eternal punishment. We may have two passages combined here again, which were originally parts of separate books with the same theme and message. But we need not let that confuse us, since the emphasis is the same. The seer appears to be so intent on describing the eventual completion of God's plan, that he blurs the distinction between heaven and earth, and the ultimate future seems to be partly earthly and partly heavenly. Perhaps this is his way of describing his insight into God's mind, since for God the whole of creation is one unified thing anyway!

21:1-8   The Third Isaiah spoke of God's plan to create a new heaven and a new earth (Is 65:17-18), with Jerusalem gloriously rebuilt after the tragedy of its military defeat. John now transfers this oracle and its imagery and applies it to the Church, which will be peaceful in the final future. The bride of 21:2 (the Church) combines the image of the people loved by God (Jr 2:2 ff.), with the great sign of the woman from chapter 12, which shows both Israel and the Church in the same scene (the woman). Now again she is the beloved and radiant bride (the figure is taken partly from the oracle of Is 62:5), as she was in the scene of the Lamb's wedding-feast in 19:7-8.

All the pain and trouble are in the past now. There is to be only peace, life and victory, symbolized by the spring of life-giving water (21:6), like the water of the messianic banquet which the Second Isaiah described in his oracle of consolation (Is 55:1; also Is 12:3 and 25:6). Jesus reigns supreme and acknowledged, the first and the last (21:5), as he was in the opening verses of the Book of Revelation (1:17).

21:9-22:5   John repeats here the imagery of himself being taken by the angel of the last septet, to see the woman (17:1 ff.). But now the woman is not the harlot Babylon (Rome), but the new heavenly city in which God and his saints are to dwell together throughout the eternity of the final age. The seer's images here come from Ezekiel's utopian vision of the new Israel (Ezk 40-48), and from the Second Isaiah's promising oracle of the newly restored Zion (Is 54:11-12). The building materials are precious metals and jewels, which symbolize unlimited excellence; the dimensions are symmetrical and perfect. Everything here is beauty, order, perfection and peace.

The heavenly city does not need a Temple or a sun or moon, because God himself lives there with his Lamb (the Father with the Son), and this is light enough—the one who called himself "the light of the world" in Jerusalem (8:12) is there! All who are good and just will be welcome, as long as they come in faith, to bring gifts of homage to the one who has overcome all evil (Is 60:11).

It may be no more than a coincidence but nevertheless it is interesting that, just as there are river- and tree-images in the opening verses of the Bible (Gn 1), there are the same images here in the last chapter of the Scripture. However, the seer has borrowed these images, not from the Priestly story of Gn 1, but from Ezekiel's oracle of the life-giving water and the fruit-bearing trees (Ez 47:1-12). However, now these images embellish not the earthly Israel, but the heavenly home of the saints, as they enjoy the light of God's presence after their trials.

The closing scene shows what has been promised: God (the Father), the Lamb (Jesus) and the faithful Christians who have persevered and now have their reward—"They shall see him face to face . . . and they shall reign forever" (22:4-5). This reminds us of Jesus' parting words to his friends, which the fourth evangelist preserved in the Last Supper Discourse: "In my Father's house there are many dwelling places . . . I shall come back to take you with me, that where I am you also may be" (Jn 14:2).

This convergence is another indication of the one mind of the beloved Disciple which underlies and unifies the basic theological message of all the Johannine writings: Jesus, the Lamb, is eternal God who dwelt among us, and those who relate to him by faith through all trials, will have his gift of God's life on earth, and after death they will see him in the eternity of the Father's heavenly presence!

E. The Epilogue (22:6-21)

All the principal personalities of Revelation have a parting word to offer in these final verses (except the Church's enemies, since they have been eliminated, in the seer's visions). We recall the Prologue (1:1-3), in which we noticed the "chain of command" as the message came from God (the Father) to Jesus, by the angel, through the seer to the Church (which means, presumably, the Ephesian Church). These all reappear now in the Epilogue. Yet there is even more here, because Jesus has a variety of new titles in these closing verses; he is the bringer of reward (22:12); the Alpha and the Omega, or the first and the last, the Beginning and the End (22:13)—which means that he shares with the Father the divine status of creator and finisher (or judge) of all. Furthermore, he is the Offspring of David and the Morning Star (22:16), both of which terms show Jesus in both cosmic and human guise. The Church itself also has special titles here, as the Bride in 22:17, and, perhaps the one in whom the Spirit dwells, or to whom the Spirit speaks, in the same verse.

There is urgency in the Epilogue also, as there was in the Prologue, since no fewer than five times in these last few verses there is mention of "soon" or "very soon." Some of these times the "soon" is in connection with the coming of Jesus (22:12, 17, 20), and the voice (presumably of divine authority, in 22:10) commands the seer not to seal up the message, since it is to become a reality soon, instead of being stored away for some unknown future. This is also why the seer presents the message, since he has received the prophetic mission to pass on to his Christian colleagues the divine message which has come to him.

After everyone has spoken his final word, the seer appears to represent the Church in 22:20, as he replies to Jesus' word, with "Maranatha!—Come, Lord Jesus!" And this prayer of the struggling Church concludes this apocalyptic message, and the Bible as well, on a note of confident expectation that God will keep his word.

Questions for Consideration and Reflection

1. What are the Old Testament texts which serve the seer as the sources of his terminology in these chapters?
2. Why is the seer so repetitious in these chapters? What are some examples of this?
3. How does the theological message of these chapters compare with that of 1 John and of the Fourth Gospel (both in similarities and differences)?
4. Which are the images which the seer repeats in these chapters from the earlier sections of Revelation?
5. Is Revelation designed to convert people to Christianity?
6. Which images and scenes of Revelation do you find most effective? Why do these impress you?
7. Now that you have made this study of Revelation, do you think that you could give a good explanation of at least its main lines, to a friend?

15

S U M M A R Y:

The Message of Saint John

"My little children,
be on your guard against idols" (1 Jn 15:21).

Now that we have followed the thread of the Beloved Disciple's teaching through the three principal works which the Johannine Christians preserved as their heritage from him, we should be able to draw some conclusions about his message.

First of all, we cannot help being impressed by the combination of variety in the literary forms of the Johannine Literature, and the underlying unity of the Apostle's message. We have seen in 1 John what has usually been called the form of an epistle, although it seems to be rather the text of a sermon or a speech, since it lacks the characteristics of a letter as recognised in the ancient world of the Apostle's time. Then there is the unique treasure which the Church possesses in the Gospel according to John. Even though it has so much in common with the works of Mark, Matthew and Luke that we often consider them together under the heading of "the four Gospels," nevertheless it stands apart from them so much in style and manner, that we can appreciate it only by seeing how it represents an original and independent mind working within the common apostolic tradition.

Apart from the narrative form and a few narrative sections which all four Gospels share, the Fourth Gospel differs from the Synoptic Gospels not only in what it says, but also in how it says it. There is a mysterious intuitive quality which this Johannine Gospel shares with 1 John, and which is not a principal feature of either the Synoptic or the Pauline writings. John always tries to bring his followers to grasp insights into the symbolic meaning of what he says. This is why, when we read the Johannine Literature, we need not only listen to the words and see the images in our mind's eye, but also must peer between the lines at what he is presupposing and implying. John does not merely give pictures of isolated incidents happening in the distant past; rather, he tries to bring his friends into a faith-commitment of their lives, to accept confidently and gratefully the fulness of the divine gift that comes to them in the person of Jesus, and to hold on to this commitment, come what may.

Revelation   Because of the close affinity which binds these former two Johannine documents together, we have to struggle a good deal to figure out the Book of Revelation and its place in the community of Saint John's followers. Its apocalyptic imagery adapts a number of Old Testament passages, and unless we are thoroughly familiar with the Old Testament, we miss these allusions, as well as the ingenious way in which the "seer" applies these passages of Scripture to the immediate situation of his Christian contemporaries in Ephesus

Probably the principal difference in the message of Revelation in comparison to 1 John and the Fourth Gospel, is that Revelation looks more to the future for salvation, whereas the other works put the emphasis rather on the "here and now" gift of divine life which Jesus gives to the Church.

Underlying Unity　　When we look at the three works in retrospect (we did not consider the Second and Third Epistles of John because they are brief and not theologically significant enough for our study here), we can recognize a certain basic unity in spite of the difference in literary forms. And this basic unity is the real message of the Apostle which we have been trying to grasp all along.

Style　　First of all, the message of Saint John comes to us in the language of figures. Since we live in the modern Western world, we probably would feel more comfortable with clear-cut, logical language which would be addressed to our rational understanding. But this is not the character of Johannine language. Instead of this, we find that we must be more flexible in becoming attuned to a pattern of parables, symbols, signs and images, which appeal to our faith on one level, and to our imagination on another level— and both at the same time. Many figures of sppech (such as "anointing" and "darkness"), and images (such as "the Word became flesh" and "the vine and the branches"), as well as even more subtle terms ("Lamb of God," "first resurrection" and "second death") are the ordinary terminology of this literature. And for this same reason we find that we have to read and re-read passages until the pattern of these figures becomes familiar enough that we see deeper into the spiritual realities which they suggest. This way of presenting spiritual realities by constantly using figurative language, is at the base of the "spiritual" quality of Johannine language.

Terminology   There is also a certain Johannine vocabulary which we find repeating itself, especially in 1 John and in the Gospel. Such words as *life; word; truth; faith/belief* (both of these terms correspond to the same word in the Greek text of the New Testament); *signs; glory; works; abide/remain; lifted up; "I AM!"* are so constant here that we can safely call them the characteristic terms of the Apostle's theological message. Of course, it would not be realistic to pretend that these words appear only in the Johannine Literature; Paul and the Synoptic evangelists use them too. But, in terms of the frequency of their occurrence, and of the special meanings which attach to them here, we can safely class these words as typically Johannine. (If we would go through the rest of the New Testament, we could also see a typically Pauline vocabulary *(justification; church; reconciliation; baptism)* and likewise some terminology which is especially prominent in the Synoptic writings *(Kingdom of God; power; Son of Man* etc.).

Dualism   This special Johannine vocabulary leads us to see the special theological emphasis which runs through all of these documents. It is the principle of dualism—the contrast, or we could even say the basic conflict—between opposite things which the teacher sees as completely incompatible. We usually see dualism as a basic feature of apocalyptic language, but it runs throughout all three of our Johannine documents. However, the two incompatible opposites are not always precisely the same things. Sometimes the conflict is between the pure Christian faith, and heresy or apostasy (1 John); in the Fourth Gospel the tension is between those who relate by faith-attachment to Jesus, and "the Jews" or "the world," who do not. In the bizarre visions of Revelation, the "seer" constantly opposes the cause of the Risen Lord and his Church, to the satanic power which he describes as that of the Roman Empire.

This dualism shows up in the frequent use of opposites in the Johannine vocabulary. There is always a tension between *flesh* and *spirit; above* and *below; life* and *death; light* and *darkness; seeing* and *blindness.* Aside from the discourse parts of the Fourth Gospel which contain this terminology, we find it also in the opposition which keeps the Christians separate from other groups, that is, from people who do not share the same faith, or from forces which could weaken this faith, or attack it. These opponents can be heretics or apostates, such as those who have fallen away from the whole apostolic belief that Jesus is nothing less than God made flesh (1 Jn 2:22). They may be Jews who reject the Christian claim that the Old Testament Scriptures point to Jesus (Jn 5:46; 8:56; 12:41). Finally, the dualism of Revelation always pits the whole earthly Church against the organized force of the pagan Roman Empire (Rv 12:1-10; 17:1-16 ff.).

This dualism of the Johannine message has both a moral aspect and an institutional one. This is why there is always a conflict here, not primarily in the lives of individual persons, or between God and Satan alone, but (in the teaching of Saint John) between the Christian Church as a whole, and outsiders who do not share its whole faith. This leads to a certain isolation for the Church, because it has to stand apart from others whose hostility threatens its life and its faith, and draw its support and strength from the spiritual resources of its own interior life, relying on the Holy Spirit, whom Jesus sent according to his promise (Jn 14:16-17; 16:8-16).

Still another aspect of this Johannine dualism is the persistent challenge which the Apostle presents to his followers, to have a truly spiritual perception, which will enable them to see beyond the limits of the ordinary, merely human sense-experience. This challenge is present in the closing words of the epistle (1 Jn 5:21), as well as in Jesus's rebuke to his unbelieving countrymen in the Fourth Gospel (Jn 3:11-12; 8:23-24; 20:29), and in the more obscure terminology of the seer's apocalypse as well (Rv 1:3; 22:7, 12). All of this comes across as an unyielding demand from the Beloved Disciple to his friends to learn and keep the divine revelation wyich has come to them through the Apostle's own witness to Jesus. These Christians have not seen Jesus but John has seen him. Likewise, the Prologue to the Fourth Gospel says that no mere human has ever seen the fulness of God, but the Only-begotten Son has come to tell us about him.

So the whole point of Christian faith, in its Johannine expression, is to know that the eternal God, who is pure heavenly spirit, has presented himself in this world in real human flesh, to offer us a share in his divine life. This is the dualism of seeing by faith and seeing merely on the level of our bodily senses.

Jesus   In all of this Johannine message the person of Jesus is, naturally, central. But it is not just any picture of him. John is remarkably consistent in presenting Jesus always as divine, glorious, fully victorious. This is one of the things that make Johannine theology different from that of the Synoptics. All three of the Synoptic evangelists take pains to show Jesus as lowly and humble, the rejected prophet and the suffering servant of God. They show him as poor, homeless, hungry and agonizing, especially as he endures hostility from his countrymen, and execution from foreigners. But the Johannine Jesus is invariably the eternal life-giving Word, the One who shows his divine glory by signs, and who is royally triumphant in death, crowned, robed in majestic purple, and even titled as king by Pilate's inscription. The couple of minor instances in which the fourth evangelist shows Jesus "grieving" for Lazarus (Jn 11:35) or "troubled" at the Last Supper (Jn 12:27), are really illustrations of Jesus' ability to overcome the limits of his humanity because of his divine understanding of the real situation.

The same divine majesty characterizes all the appearances of Jesus in Revelation. From the first scene of the opening chapter, Jesus is radiant with the features of divine knowledge and power. As the Lamb, he is the victorious mediator of God's eternal plan for the world and for the Church (Rv 19:11-21).

We can see that this picture of Jesus, always radiant in divine glory and victory, before as well as after his Passion and Resurrection, would both uplift and challenge John's Christian followers, who had never seen Jesus in the flesh. But a Lord who could make such an impression on the Apostle, should certainly be worth believing in. There is nothing maudlin or sentimental or uncertain, about the image of Jesus that we see in all of these Johannine writings.

The Church   As for the Church itself, this is also a principal theme of Saint John's teaching—even though the word never occurs in the Fourth Gospel or in the First Epistle. But, whether the word is there or not, the thing that matters is that these books contain the Beloved Disciple's message to his Christian disciples; and they make up the local church in Ephesus. True enough, the problems which face the

Christians of Ephesus may be not entirely the same as the ones which the other local churches have to handle. But, even so, the message of Revelation is more comprehensive, since it deals fundamentally with the relationship of the whole Church to all of its enemies, especially to the Roman Empire and its satellite kingdoms.

In all of these Johannine books the word of God's message comes through the Apostle's teaching, to Christians who are living under pressure. The sources of the pressure are quite varied, partly internal, but mostly coming from outside. These pressures are multiple, whether they are heresies of apostate Christians, the animosity of unconverted Jews, or the sexual licentiousness and pagan idolatry of the Roman Empire. In the face of all of these hostile forces, it is understandable that John has a difficult task, as he tries to encourage these converts to retain a life-style and an attitude which will set them apart from most of their neighbors and countrymen. Such isolation makes them feel helpless, thrown on the defensive and strongly tempted to compromise or abandon a faith which demands nothing less than their total commitment. It might not be so difficult if he could offer them some tangible guarantee that it is all worth-while. But all that he can offer them is a picture of an executed Lord who has worked signs and claimed to be equal to the eternal Father, promises to his followers an indwelling Paraclete and a Lord who shows his Risen Body to his bewildered friends, and appears as a Lamb, a Lion and a King.

The Mystery   All in all, as we saw at the beginning of our study, the Beloved Disciple's message is not so much a presentation of facts or opinions which he submits for analysis; rather it is his authoritative apostolic witness to the supernatural mystery of divine life offered to men in a human form to which they can relate. Only the eyes—and ears—of a trusting faith will be able to accept and appreciate this witness, and identify with the gift that it promises.

Present and Future   This brings us to one of the major differences of perspective which we find within the Johannine corpus, namely the variant emphasis regarding the earthly and heavenly phases of the Church. There is no great difficulty in seeing that both 1 John and the

Gospel According to John speak mostly of the earthly life of Christians, so that in these documents there is an almost exclusive concentration on the life of faith under pressure. The people who received these messages could hardly miss the point that the teacher wanted them to feel the consolation and assurance that came from knowing the absent Lord by faith, and recognizing the abiding presence of the Holy Spirit in their hearts. This should buoy them up so much that they would become indifferent to threats, seductions or errors arising from outside their own community, and make them realize that they share God's animating presence which lives within them. For them, eternity is *now*! They already have heaven on earth!

The theological thrust of Revelation is different from this, however. Like the apocalyptic prophecies of the Old Testament, the seer's main message to his friends was an invitation to look more to the promise of a victory which awaited them in the ultimate future, rather than to the consolation which they would want to feel in the present time. Indeed, the present time (in John's day) offered precious little consolation to Christians, since they had been ostracized, ridiculed and martyred since Jesus' day, through the time of Stephen, Peter and Paul, and up to the time of the Beloved Disciple himself. Nero had been viciously hostile in the 60's, and now Domitian was renewing the unlivable misery of Nero's anti-Christian campaign.

These developments led the seer to bring his prophetic message, centered in the Lord's guarantee that their earthly suffering would earn a heavenly joy. This is why we see the principally futuristic orientation which is the dominant emphasis of Revelation and its message of promise.

Theological Unity   Nevertheless, we could become preoccupied with these differences and thereby miss the fact that even here there is an underlying Johannine unity. Apocalypse, Gospel, or Epistle, all of these call urgently for persevering commitment in trusting faith, to the full mystery of divine life which God has given to Christians in Jesus. This is the Church's work for the earthly present—to see and hold this precious gift in the face of all odds, even if it requires Christians to undergo the death of martyrdom. It could hardly be more than what Jesus did. But Christians should be able to face such trials with calm, knowing what Jesus told his friends at the Last Supper—that he will send them the Holy Spirit, and that he will come and take them with himself to the Father's presence. Even the seer of Revelation had a privileged glimpse of the martyrs and of their reward (Rv 7:13-17; 12:11), which is the eternal enjoyment of God's heavenly approval of their faithful testimony.

So the Johannine view of the Church is both earthly for the present, and heavenly for the future. But the consolations of the present time should not—and must not—deceive. The trials remain, and will continue, as long as faith must deal with unfaith. But, if we could only appreciate the gift which animates and sustains the Church's earthly present—trials and all—then martyrdom would be welcome, since it would bring us even more of the same consolations—and without any prospect of having it come to an end.

The Rest of the New Testament   Ordinarily we think of our Christian faith and its teachings as a whole, and as a general rule we are not accustomed to recognize what is specifically from the Scripture and what is from the later years of Christian tradition, as it grew from the days of the biblical writers. Likewise, when we speak of the Bible, and especially of the New Testament, we are likely to see it as a composite, without distinguishing what is from Paul, or from the Synoptics, or from the teaching of Saint John. However, in order to draw together our conclusions about the Johannine message, we need to see, at least in broad strokes, how it relates to the rest of the New Testament, i.e. to the Synoptics and to the teaching of Saint Paul, as we have it in his letters.

Naturally, all the New Testament authors share the common apostolic Gospel, which is centered in the Paschal Mystery of Jesus' Passion and Glorification, and in the coming of the Holy Spirit to the Church. Even though the narrative of these scenes comes in the closing chapters of all four Gospels, nevertheless, it is the core and base of the message which the Apostles preached. We see this in the speeches of Peter and the other Apostles in the first chapters of the Acts of the Apostles (Ac 2; 3; 4; 5; 7; 10). Paul was "grafted on" to the apostolic college later, but he preached the same message (Ac 13; 1 Cor 15), as he told the gentiles that God had brought a new age by conquering evil in the death and glorification of Jesus. In this the Scriptures are fulfilled, and God's victory is available to all men by faith in the Risen Lord.

The variations of the apostolic message show up in the different literary forms of the Synoptics and of Paul. Whereas Paul applied this Gospel by writing occasional letters to his converts about situations which arose in their Christian life and experience, Mark was the one who forged a new path by originating a brand-new literary form, which we now know familiarly as the Gospel. Eventually, Matthew's and Luke's Gospels came to be based on this new one that Mark had produced, as these later evangelists adapted Mark's contribution to their own purposes. These Synoptic evangelists combined the apostolic Gospel of the Paschal Mystery, with Jesus' own preaching, which was his Gospel of the Kingdom of God. Jesus challenged his countrymen to live according to the message of God's saving lordship, as it was present in the full Jewish tradition, even though the leaders of Israel had distorted it, and failed to teach their people the correct meaning of the Law and the Prophets. These Synoptic evangelists wanted to show to their Christian friends the background of the Paschal Mystery, and the connection between it and Jesus' Public Ministry, and also between it and Israel's earlier tradition. In this they surpassed Paul, who continually preached the Paschal Mystery, but had little or nothing to say in his letters about Jesus' Public Ministry, or about his remote origins.

Paul had written his letters in the early 50's and the early 60's, and the Synoptic evangelists had produced their Gospels (and the Acts of the Apostles) in the two decades after that. So by the time the Johannine writings appeared, they were comparatively late additions to the growing collection of Christian documents. Yet, they were basically continuous with the earlier writings, because of the fundamental sameness which joins the Johannine message to that of the earlier New Testament preachers. Jesus is still central, in his Public Ministry, his power to work miracles, and in his Passion and Glorification.

Nevertheless, the special Johannine independence shows in the perspective of eternity, which shows Jesus coming to earth, not merely from Adam or Abraham (as Matthew and Luke have shown), but from God's eternity, as the Word made Flesh. Likewise, the Johannine Jesus calls for faith not in God as the ruler of the kingdom, but in himself as the Word and Son who offers God's life to believers *now*. And, whereas the three Synoptics and Paul present Jesus as a man uniquely sent by God and in whom God lives, works and speaks in a new way, John is unequivocal in presenting Jesus as nothing less than eternal, and divine, as creative and as life-giving as the Father is. The Synoptic Jesus is governed by the Spirit of God; the Johannine Jesus gives the Holy Spirit, just as the Father does. Furthermore, although the Synoptics show Jesus as the suffering servant and the rejected prophet, John's picture of him is invariably triumphant, omniscient and omnipotent, even as men tragically fail to appreciate him or relate to him on the level of faith.

In the area of Jesus' teaching, John simplifies it. There are no Parables of the Kingdom, and no Sermon on the Mount in the Johannine message. The only demands Jesus makes in the Johannine writings are that men should believe in him as the Word made flesh, and that they should love one another according to Jesus' own example. This Johannine ethic is at once more simple and more all-embracing than the various directives which Paul gives in his letters, or those which the Synoptics place on the lips of Jesus.

In retrospect, we see an amazing combination of similarities and differences. There can be no doubt that the followers of the Beloved Disciple must have been impressed by his message, with the deeper and more spiritual insights into the meaning of Jesus' works and words which are its special hallmark. This makes the Johannine Jesus identical with the Lord of the earlier apostolic preachers and of the Synoptics. At the same time, it shows more the divinity of Jesus, his offer of divine life, his call for a faith in himself that will accept martyrdom, and his assurance that the Holy Spirit will be his gift to his believing followers. Beyond this, the apocalyptic visions of Revelation promise, in their own bizarre way, the ultimate victory of Jesus and of his persecuted Church over all evil and all attackers, so that heaven's final bliss will be the eventual reward of disciples' faith and endurance.

The Message and Our Situation

The Beloved Disciple's message comes across to us as both a consolation and a challenge. It is uncompromisingly the language of committed faith. Certainly it is a mistake to see in these Johannine writings nothing more than a history of the past or a prediction of the future. We could never do full justice to John's message if we would try to organize it into a collection of abstract statements of fact. All of this is simply because the main point of the Apostle's teaching is not a telling, or an informing, but an urging and an encouraging. John urges his friends to live according to the full faith-dimension that their lives are capable of reaching. To do this, then or now, means letting God do what he has set out to do, and communicate himself to our humanity. This does not change God, but it certainly changes us. It moves us from a merely earthly and sensual, short-range life-style, to a more deep-seeing level, and this makes us constantly aware of the divine Word which lives in us, and of the Holy Spirit who teaches and comforts us.

The language of faith which John speaks in these writings invites us to read between the lines, beyond parables, symbols, signs and images, and allow ourselves to be addressed by God who comes to us. As we do this, a potential opens in the depth of our souls, and the fulness of God's own life pours into it. Our eager acceptance of his gift is our faith-response to John's faith-message. Our life is spiritualized beyond our expectation.

Beyond this the relevance of Saint John's message consists in the fact that he offers us a religion that is fully and truly divine. A mere intellectual analysis will never give us the understanding that John calls "the light." Likewise, a simplified humanism which fails to give God credit for the totality of his gift to us in Jesus, offers us nothing that could inspire anyone to martyrdom or even to courageous endurance. But the full truth that the apostates failed to grasp, and that Jesus' own countrymen were unable to perceive, utterly surpasses the level of merely human terminology. This fully divine religion that John urges his friends to maintain, dignifies and uplifts our humanity, as we ponder the lengths to which God has gone to bring us to himself, and himself to us.

This faith-view of God's working and of his plan, together with the deeper perception which goes beyond our sense-experience to know God's self-gift, makes our daily life peaceful. The absent Lord's gift of the Paraclete consoles and encourages us, teaching us throughout our life-pilgrimage to live the mystery to which we have been initiated. The short-range frustrations which come from shallow earth-mindedness, pass away now, and we become accustomed to savoring the gentleness of the indwelling Holy Spirit. Our eucharistic experience becomes a sharing in the loaves-event, and in the conversation in the Upper Room. We learn to avoid the mistake of Mary at the tomb, or of Thomas on the eighth day—the mistake of trying to fit the Father and his lifted-up Son into earth-bound expectations, which can never convey the reality of their working.

Promise

The same perspective promises even more for the future. Even though we do not have the same prospect nowadays of dying by martyrdom, we feel nevertheless the thrill and the expectation of being admitted eventually to the presence that the seer's powerful imagery can only suggest. For those who are guided by John's teaching, death is a welcome passage to the completion of what baptism has begun and what the eucharist has nourished. The inner peace of the present will be even greater, so that we see our earthly faith-life as a day-by-day preparation for what will be even better in the end, when the Risen Lord brings us to it.

EPILOGUE

One of the many new emphases in the Church since the Second Vatican Council, has been the re-discovery of the Holy Scriptures. We could hardly say that the Church did not know or use the Bible before the Council, but we must acknowledge that the Scriptures did not get as much attention as they might have gotten. There were many reasons for this situation, of course, but nevertheless we have moved, together and ecclesially, to a new era in which the Scriptures will, we expect, be the familiar and principal source of spirituality for God's people that they should be. The greater prominence of the Liturgy of the Word in the Mass and in all the sacramental rites shows us that the Church is now moving in this direction. The study of theology and of spirituality nowadays simply presupposes a thorough grasp of at least the main lines of the Bible, and its principal theological themes.

There is always the danger, however, that our study of theology or of the Bible may be too academic. This has often happened, and this kind of situation does not sanctify people or feed their spirits with the divine presence which the Holy Scriptures can offer. On the other hand, it is no better to read or hear the Scriptures with a complete lack of understanding. People in general are better educated nowadays, but their spiritual growth must keep pace with their progress in the other areas of their lives. Therefore, we need to overcome a fear which would make us hesitate to approach the Bible because we might feel defeated by its complexities, even before we would open it.

Undoubtedly, we have had so much genuine progress in biblical study in the present generation, that we would make a tragic mistake if we would deprive ourselves of these advances by failing to take on the project. We feel a certain reluctance, but we should undertake the task anyway, in the Lord's name and for the sake of our own souls.

The basic purpose of these reflections has been to offer a sample of the benefits of scientific biblical study without the burden of unnecessary technical details. These additional details are readily available in academic commentaries, but they are usually complicated and not designed primarily to feed our spiritual hunger. We need, therefore, some studies that will translate technical exegesis of the Bible, into effective spiritual nourishment for our contemporary generation. This is what these reflections were designed to offer. If they have helped us to benefit from scientific biblical study in a way that gives us even a small taste of the joy that the Scriptures offer, and especially if they have at least opened a window onto the richness of Saint John's message, the effort has been worth-while. Now,

> "To the One that sits on the throne,
>   and to the Lamb,
> be praise and honor, glory and might,
>   forever and ever! (Rv 5:13)

An Interesting Thought

The publication you have just finished reading is part of the apostolic efforts of the Society of St. Paul of the American Province. A small, unique group of priests and brothers, the members of the Society of St. Paul propose to bring the message of Christ to men through the communications media while living the religious life.

If you know a young man who might be interested in learning more about our life and mission, ask him to contact the Vocation Office in care of the Society of St. Paul, Alba House Community, Canfield, Ohio 44406 (phone 216/533-5503). Full information will be sent without cost or obligation. You may be instrumental in helping a young man to find his vocation in life.
An interesting thought.